FROM ROOMMATES TO SOULMATES

IN 30 DAYS OR LESS, GUARANTEED!

FROM ROOMMATES TO SOULMATES

IN 30 DAYS OR LESS, GUARANTEED!

"THE KEYS TO CREATING A PHENOMENAL MARRIAGE BY DESIGN"

DAVID RISPOLI

XULON ELITE

Xulon Press Elite
555 Winderley Pl, Suite 225
Maitland, FL 32751
407.339.4217
www.xulonpress.com

© 2023 by David Rispoli

All rights reserved solely by the author. The author guarantees all contents are original and do not infringe upon the legal rights of any other person or work. No part of this book may be reproduced in any form without the permission of the author.

Due to the changing nature of the Internet, if there are any web addresses, links, or URLs included in this manuscript, these may have been altered and may no longer be accessible. The views and opinions shared in this book belong solely to the author and do not necessarily reflect those of the publisher. The publisher therefore disclaims responsibility for the views or opinions expressed within the work.

Paperback ISBN-13: 978-1-66288-975-2
Ebook ISBN-13: 978-1-66288-976-9

Acknowledgements

I want to give credit and a sincere thank you to bestselling author, international relationship coach, my mentor and friend, Mort Fertel. Mort's Marriage Fitness program has helped saved thousands of relationships around the world. Much of the wisdom found in these pages has been wisdom imparted to me from Mort. Because of Mort's leadership in my life, I have had two phenomenal marriages.

I want to thank and acknowledge the hundreds of couples from all around the world who have trusted me to help them when their marriage was in crisis.

I want to thank my beautiful wife, Jennifer. She is my new soul mate and best friend who has embraced these principles and given me the opportunity to love again.

I want to thank Cathy, my first soul mate, for encouraging me to write this book and help others to create phenomenal marriages by design, and to live and finish life with no regrets.

Table of Contents

Preface Is This Book Hogwash? ix

Introduction As a Married Couple, Live in the Moment 1

Chapter 1 From Roommates to Soulmates 9

Chapter 2 Marriage By Design 17

Chapter 3 The Marriage Manifesto 27

Chapter 4 Belief Systems 35

Chapter 5 Respect 45

Chapter 6 Communication 55

Chapter 7 Date Night, Hobbies & Volunteering: The Trifecta of Togetherness 67

Chapter 8 Touch & Sexual Intimacy 75

Chapter 9 Giving Presents and Presence 83

Chapter 10 Arguing and Conflict Resolution 91

Chapter 11 Protecting the Marriage 99

Epilogue 107

Endnotes 111

What People are Saying about David Rispoli
(The Marriage Coach) 113

PREFACE
Is This Book Hogwash?

THROUGHOUT MY LIFE I have been particularly blessed in that people have always been unusually kind to me. It is very seldom I have encountered someone who is rude or confrontational. I am not sure why this is the case. Maybe it is because of my size, perhaps it's my demeanor, maybe it is the way I carry myself, or maybe it is my profession.

However, this one day, I experienced a woman who really was downright rude. I was on a plane flying back from Dallas, Texas. I had just given a speech to executives on the importance of prioritizing their marriages above their businesses. I have this conviction that if you have a winning business but are failing in your marriage you are losing. I was working in my aisle seat on the book you are now reading, minding my own business.

The middle-aged woman in the window seat next to me asked what I was doing. I shared I was working on the final touches of a book I was writing. Her response was less than encouraging.

When I told her the title, *From Roommates to Soulmates in 30 Days or Less, Guaranteed*, she blurted out, "That is hogwash, absolute hogwash. Impossible! What are you, a magician, or a con artist? Are you joking?"

Her barrage of why it was impossible continued the rest of the flight. Sometimes loudly, drawing the attention of flight attendants and people sitting around us. This angry, smitten woman wanted no part of a conversation about relationships. She was completely turned off.

I realize that the title of this book is quite a claim. At worse, it sounds like hype or a marketing ploy to sell books. At best, it sounds too good to be true. After all, if it took a married couple, five, ten, twenty, thirty, or more years to get their relationship to a "roommate" place, how in the world can things get turned around in thirty days?

How in the world can things get turned around in thirty days?
What if you married the wrong person?
What if your soulmate is still someplace out there?

I can tell you beyond a shadow of doubt, that you and your spouse can have a soulmate relationship in less than thirty days. I have observed this phenomenon for the past two decades in my coaching practice. I have seen couples on the brink of divorce make miraculous recoveries. I have seen good marriages become great marriages. I have seen individuals whose spouses were 100 percent checked out of their marriages, single-handedly, love their spouses back into the marriage using many of the principles I am going to share with you in this book. The truth is the pathway from roommate to soulmate is much easier than you might think. In this book, I am going to show you the path and I promise you it can revolutionize your marriage.

Right from the start, I want you to know that the principles you will read about in this book are well-researched. A host of scientific peer-reviewed research exists to support the claims I will make in this book. Having said this, please remember, I am not some academic professor, teaching his students how to build a successful business in a classroom, while never having run a business myself. Haven't we all had that experience? Someone will get in front of us professing to be a guru or an expert, but they have no real experience at the thing that they are teaching.

The principles you will read about in this book are principles I have not only shared with thousands of individuals and couples in my coaching business, but I have personally applied over decades to my own successful marriages. I say marriages because I have had two wildly successful marriages. I am widowed and will share more of this story in a moment. I know that they work. I have seen them work for literally thousands of couples around the world, I have seen them work in my own marriage and I know they will work for you.

"Hogwash, Magician, Con-Artist," call it what you want, let's get started in our transition from roommates to soulmates! Thank you for joining me on this journey.

INTRODUCTION
As a Married Couple, Live in the Moment

THERE ARE SEVERAL reasons you may have picked up this book. Maybe you were intrigued by the title. Maybe you are engaged to be married and you want to ensure you create a phenomenal future with your fiancé. Maybe you are in a good marriage, and you want to take it to the next level. Maybe you have been married for years but the fire and passion have left the marriage and you are trying to reignite it. Maybe you are tired of living as roommates and truly want to pivot your relationship to a better place. Maybe you are in a situation where your spouse has checked out and you are desperate to win them back.

Regardless of your reason for picking up this book, I want to thank you for making the investment in your relationship. I especially want to thank you for giving me the opportunity to go on this journey with you. My purpose for writing this book is to help people create beautiful marriages by design, have no relational regrets, and have the phenomenal marriage of their dreams.

I love helping couples transition their relationships from roommate status to soulmates. Through the years, I have had the opportunity to work with hundreds of couples from all around the world at different stages of the marital journey. I have earned the reputation of being one of the most experienced and successful marriage coaches in the world. My goal is to help a million people save their marriages and to create the marriage of their dreams. I am accomplishing this mission one marriage at a time, and I am so honored to have the opportunity to help you with your marriage.

To this end, I would like to share a little of my own journey so that you fully understand the perspective from which this book was written. The journey starts in an unusual place for a book written on marriage. It begins in the living room of a fifty-two-year-old man who had just been told he has less than six months to live. Ed had just been diagnosed with throat cancer. I was twenty-seven years old and had recently volunteered to be a hospice chaplain. I had agreed to this volunteer position because hospice chaplains could have their student loans deferred. I had no idea what hospice was, and I had no idea what deferred meant. All I knew was that on my pastor's salary, I would now not have to make the minimum monthly student loan payments. I subsequently learned I would be visiting people who had been told that they had six months or less to live. That's it. That's all I knew.

Ed was the first person I visited as a hospice chaplain. He had retired from a very successful and lucrative career in the insurance industry. Six weeks earlier, he had sold his business with plans to travel the world and play golf. Now, he was sitting in front of me in his living room overcome with pain, anger, and grief. Ed spoke through a tracheotomy tube. He did not understand how a good God would let this happen. He lamented at the unfairness of being struck with this terrible cancer at fifty-two years of age. He was furious he had worked so hard and sacrificed so much only for his life to end this way. He was angry at God, his family, his doctor, and at me.

Ed wanted answers. I had none. At twenty-seven, I had never lost anyone close to me. I had received no formal hospice training and was ill-prepared for this visit. I did the only thing I could do. I sat there and cried with Ed. I agreed with him. It was unfair.

At the end of our visit, I said the only thing I could think to say. "Ed, you are still here. Don't become so consumed with dying, that you forget to live today. Ed, remember to live today."

Amazingly, Ed took my advice. He started to live every day. He became less consumed with dying and more consumed with living. He told all three of his children he loved them. This was the first time he had ever articulated these words to his children. He was reconciled with a brother he had not talked to in over a decade.

Ed became softer and kinder with his wife. The two of them were able to take several trips and he later shared these were the best days of his life. Ed had taken the advice to remember to live today to heart. He began to live life to its fullest one day at a time…maybe for the first time in his life. I visited Ed on a weekly basis and our friendship deepened.

About six months after meeting Ed, he became totally bedbound. The cancer started to take its course and Ed's life. I would now visit with Ed in his bedroom where he spent most his time in the hospice bed. Through all of this downward spiral in his health, Ed remained positive. One day, as we were finishing our visit, Ed called me back into the room. As I sat on his bed, he pulled me close to his mouth.

I said, "Ed what is it?"

Ed reached up to his tracheotomy tube and put his finger on the hole that enabled him to speak. When he spoke, he said these five amazing words. Five words that would change my life.

He said, "Dave, remember to live today."

These same words I had spoken to him 6 months earlier; he was now speaking to me. I had spoken these words to over a dozen other hospice patients in the past six months, but no one had ever spoken those words to me. They seared my heart. At that moment, it occurred to me that I had not been living. I had been waiting to live. I kept thinking I would live…

when my career took off.

> when my kids were older.

>> when the conditions were right.

>>> when I had more money and a nicer home.

All these excuses had kept me from truly living.

At that moment, I decided to remember to live today, every day. I made the decision to squeeze every last drop out of life, living every day as if it was my last. I made the decision to not take life for granted and to remember to live today, every day.

That visit was the last time I saw Ed. He died in his sleep that very evening. However, the gift he gave me truly changed the trajectory of my life. Now you might be thinking:

- *How does this relate me and my marriage? Or,*
- *What does this have to do with moving from roommates to soulmates in thirty days or less?*
- *You might be thinking why is this story in a book about marriage?*

The story does not end with Ed. Fast forward a quarter of a century to September 2017. Now I am sitting on the hospital bed of another fifty-two-year-old. Like Ed, this person has cancer. This person was not a hospice patient though, this fifty-two-year-old was my best friend, my soulmate, and the most beautiful person I have ever known. Her name was Cathy, my wife. Cathy had been diagnosed with stage 4 lung cancer that had spread to her liver, lymph nodes, and brain. Her diagnosis had been a shock to us because she had no symptoms and had never smoked a day in her life.

In April of 2016, Cathy returned to the gym vowing to get into the best shape of her life. In quick order, she felt better than she had ever felt. In February of 2017, she thought she had pulled a muscle in her back. She had a little pain in her back, so we called our family doctor and he suggested we come in for an X-ray. That evening he called me and asked me to bring Cathy back in to do another X-ray. The doctor did not like what he saw and wanted to take more pictures. Within forty-eight hours, on February 14 of 2017, we would learn her diagnosis.

For the first twenty-four hours, we were devastated and shocked. The doctor told us that Cathy had six months to live. After the shock wore off, we looked at each other and remembered the mantra that had governed our entire marriage.

Remember to live today.

We had lived every day to the fullest. We both acknowledged how blessed we had been. We had no regrets. We had no, "We wish we would have" or "We should have" or "Why didn't we?". We had raised three amazing children who were super successful adults. We had traveled the world, and we had lived and loved every single day. We had careers that we loved, and we had made a difference. We had great friends and a great church, and we had learned the power of generosity. We simply had no regrets.

We knew God could heal Cathy of cancer and that we could trust Him. We also knew that if for whatever reason He chose not to heal her, we would continue to trust Him. We decided right then and there that we would fight cancer, continue to live, continue to love, continue to trust God and to remember to live today.

We had made another decision prior to our marriage that would prove to be life-altering. We had decided that before we got married, we would go through some sort of pre-marriage counseling. Cathy found a course called *Marriage Fitness*. *Marriage Fitness* was a six-week marriage enrichment program that was telephone driven and developed by Mort Fertel.

This teleconference was the most eye-opening relationship training I had ever received.

During this course, we learned what it would take to keep a lifelong connection. We learned the power of putting love first and focusing on keeping a loving connection. We learned the skills to create a phenomenal marriage. Between the lessons learned from Mort and the life philosophy we learned from my friend Ed; we were equipped to live a marriage with purpose and by design that ultimately left us in a place of no regrets when faced with the worst this life had to offer.

We were on vacation in Destin, Florida when Cathy passed. Everyone, including the two of us, believed she was beating cancer. It had been 26 weeks since her diagnosis. She had not spent a single day in the hospital, had few symptoms, and just a little pain. During those 26 weeks, we traveled the world. We were in five different countries and beaches all around the world. When we were on those beaches we talked mostly about life, and we lived in the moment.

Live in the Moment

We talked about our life, our children, our marriage, and the future. Cathy encouraged me to write this book. Cathy encouraged me to continue to live, love, and trust God even if she passed. Cathy encouraged me to find love again in this world in the event she died.

Our last hours together were as amazing as our entire marriage had been. Sitting next to her on her hospital bed, I asked her if she was afraid. She said *no*.

Then she said, "God is so good. I love you, Scruff." (Scruff was her nickname for me).

She died peacefully in my arms at fifty-two years of age. We had no regrets. Thanks to the lesson we learned from Ed, we lived every day to the fullest.

This book is a manual on what I have learned about love and marriage. It is a manual on how to create a soulmate relationship. I know that the claim in thirty days sounds absurd, but the truth is, it happens the instant you decide to begin to change your behaviors. My lab has been my own life and the thousands of couples I have worked with through the years.

I know...

- *what it is to be in a broken relationship where nothing seems to work and both partners lose hope.*
- *what it is to be in a hurting relationship where you think you are doing everything you possibly can, and it still is not working.*
- *what is to be in a relationship where you have lost all hope.*

I *also* know...

- *what it is to be in a phenomenal relationship.*
- *what it is to be in a marriage where you wake up every day and it truly is great.*

This book provides the roadmap to creating a PHENOMENAL MARRIAGE. The tagline of this book is *Creating a Marriage by Design* because I have learned great marriages are not accidents. They don't just happen; they happen by design.

This book will work for you regardless of what stage your relationship is in today. *If you are not married yet,* this book can serve as a wonderful pre-marital blueprint to create and keep the marriage of your dreams. I have applied these same principles to my second phenomenal marriage.

The principles in this book will also work for you if you are in a good marriage but would like it to be in a phenomenal marriage. These relationship principles can transform a good marriage into a great marriage.

Finally, this book will also work for you if your marriage is in a broken place today. I have used these principles to help save hundreds of marriages. I know these principles work because I have lived them and am living them today.

I especially want to thank you for reading this book and making an investment in your marriage. I also thank you for having a desire to not settle for a mediocre marriage but for your willingness to design the marriage of your dreams.

If you follow the principles in this book, you are destined to have a phenomenal marriage. Follow the principles in this book and you will have a great marriage with your soulmate. Whether you are planning on getting married, have a great marriage, or have a broken marriage, read this book with anticipation and hope.

The best is yet to come for you and your spouse!

CHAPTER 1

From Roommates to Soulmates

THE TAGLINE OF St. Louis Marriage Coaching is "Turning Roommates into Soulmates." I have used this tagline for my marriage coaching business for close to twenty years. I receive a lot of feedback on it and most of my clients love it. When couples finish working with me, they frequently report they feel more like soulmates than roommates. I never explored this phenomenon. While I knew it was a positive thing because these coaching clients all made referrals and said wonderful things about my coaching practice, I never questioned the tagline.

Then the time came for me to write this book. My desire was to write a book on how I help roommates become soulmates. I soon discovered a huge problem: people have all kinds of ideas about what the word *soulmate* means. I began to ask people, "When you think of the word soulmate, what comes to mind?" I surveyed several hundred people over a two-year period.

To my surprise, I discovered the concept of "soulmates" was one of the driving forces behind marital dissatisfaction. In fact, misunderstanding who a soulmate is may be one of the major problems with marriage today. Many people have such unrealistic ideas about "soulmates" that they ditch their marriage in search of this holy grail called their "soulmate." How often do you hear people say their affair partner is their soulmate? I hear it all the time. How often have you heard people long for a deeper more fulfilling soulmate-like relationship? I hear this all the time. I realized it was time to start talking and writing about the concept of soulmates.

According to a 2021 survey conducted by *YouGov*, 60 percent of Americans believe in the idea of soulmates[1]. The challenge comes when we begin to dig deeper into what people believe about soulmates. For some people, soulmates are passionate lovers who can't take their hands off each other. For others, soulmates are so intellectually connected they constantly complete one another's thoughts and sentences.

Some assume soulmates are so emotionally connected that when one of them hurts, the other hurts, and when one of them is experiencing joy, the other experiences joy. These connected at-the-hip soulmates travel through life enjoying the same hobbies, interests, music, food taste, and travel passions. An overwhelming majority of people believe we are destined to find our soulmate. With a definition like this, it is little wonder our divorce rate is 50 percent.

This romanticized concept of soulmates dates clear back to 385 BC. The Greek Philosopher Plato wrote a work called Symposium[2]. In it, he described humans as creatures with four arms, four legs, and two faces. Because humans had become so proud, the God Zeus cut them in half as punishment. Humans were now destined to walk the earth searching for their other half. When they find their other half, it was said they found their soulmate.

Hollywood perpetuates this concept of soulmates. Frequently, when characters are portrayed in a positive relational light, only the positive passionate aspects of the relationship are highlighted. This leaves the impression that the sizzle reel we see on the screen is the real thing. Whose marriage can compare to a Hollywood sizzle reel? The same is true of social media. Couples put their best pictures on Facebook. This can give others the impression that things are better than what they are in reality. We compare our ordinary marriages with our neighbor's exciting fakebook marriage laden with trips, gifts, fun, and excitement.

The Soulmate Connection

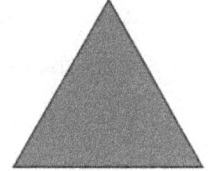

Passionate/Physical   Intimate/Emotional

Soulmate

A soulmate connection transcends or goes beyond the emotional and intimate passionate, and physical aspects of the relationship. Imagine a relationship as an equilateral triangle where all three sides have the same length.

The left side of this triangle represents the passionate and physical aspects of the relationship. This includes touch, closeness, warmth, sex, passion, energy, excitement, and all the things that go with keeping the relationship exciting.

The second side of the triangle represents the intimate, emotional aspects of the relationship. This includes how we communicate and support one another, how we are present in the relationship, and how we are growing in the relationship.

The third side connecting the two is the soulmate line. This is the line that is rooted in our values, our commitment to the marriage, and the essence of who we are as human beings. It is somewhat spiritual in that it is much deeper than the physical and emotional. It has nothing to do with feelings, emotions, or the capacity to be a great communicator, listener, or lover. It is a connection on the soul level that carries us through all the seasons of a marriage. Even when a couple is struggling with the other two sides of the triangle, this is the part of the triangle that says, "Don't give up, keep trying, it can get better." It is the connection that is rooted on a soul level.

This soulmate connection does not ignore the importance of the other two triangle sides. This book will address the physical side and the emotional side of the relationship triangle. It acknowledges there may be seasons where those areas ebb and flow with time, but the essence and core of the relationship is grounded and rooted in values. It is rooted in the promises made the day the couple married. For many couples, the promises were something like, "To have and to hold from this day forward, through good times and bad times, through sickness and health, through richer or poorer, till death do us part." This is a soulmate connection.

Notice, most of us never said,

- "I will stay married as long as you are a rock star in bed."
- Or, "I will stay married as long as you are a great communicator or listener."
- Or, "I will stay married as long as you make me happy."

Have you ever made one of these statements?

For many of the couples I work with, marriage renewal happens the instant couples make the decision to return to their wedding day soulmate promises. These promises were the glue intended to keep the marriage together, but many couples have not thought of these vows for years. Soulmate connection begins to return as we return to these promises.

Your Soulmate Connection Begins

- ♥ Find your wedding vows.
- ♥ Find the promises you made the day you said Yes to one another.

- ♥ Regardless of where things have been, regardless of how you feel about them, regardless of what is broken, decide to begin to live in these promises.
- ♥ Type them out, print them out, put them on your wall, or make them the screen saver on your phone or computer.
- ♥ This is the soulmate connection.

My wife Jennifer and I have a great physical connection. She is a beautiful woman, and I am told by others weekly that when I married her, I out punted my coverage. We have a great emotional connection, too. We both feel seen and heard in our marriage. However, the thing that binds us together and makes us unstoppable is our soulmate connection. We realize there will be seasons where the physical and emotional will ebb and flow, but the cornerstone and foundation of our marriage are the promises we made to one another the day we married. This is a soulmate connection.

I would like to close this chapter by sharing a story that illustrates the power of the soulmate connection. It is the story of Robertson McQuilkin.

Robertson McQuilkin had followed in his father's footsteps and became the President of Columbia Bible College and Seminary in 1968. Under his leadership, the school doubled enrollment and transitioned to university status. Columbia had become one of the most prestigious Bible colleges in the United States. McQuilkin's leadership was talked about in corporate America circles, and he was a stellar example to the many students graduating from Columbia.

In 1990, his wife Muriel developed Alzheimer's disease. He and Muriel had met when they were both students at Columbia. Dr. McQuilkin had eight years left in his contract with Columbia and many of his friends and family encouraged him to put Muriel in an institution where she could receive around-the-clock care.

No one would have faulted McQuilkin had he made the decision to finish his career and visit his wife daily in a long-term care facility. After all, he was young and was looking at the brightest days of his career. However, he made the decision to retire immediately. His resignation speech to Columbia has been heard by millions of people around the world on YouTube. Here is just a small piece of it:

> "I haven't in my life experienced easy decision-making on major decisions, but one of the simplest and clearest decisions that I have had to make is this one because circumstances dictated it. Muriel now, in the last couple of months seems to be almost happy when she is with me and almost never happy when she is not with me. In fact, she seems to feel trapped, becomes very fearful, sometimes almost terrified, and when she can't get to me there can be anger, and she is in distress. However, when I am with her, she is happy and contented. And so, I must be with her at all times, and you see it's not only that, I promised in sickness in health till death do us part and I am a man of my word but as I have said publicly it's the only fair thing, after all, she has sacrificed for me for forty years, to make my life possible. So, if I cared for her for forty years, I would still be in debt. However, there is much more. It's not that I have to. It's that I get to. I love her very dearly. She's a delight. It is a great honor to care for such a wonderful person.[3]"

The connection Robertson and Muriel had was truly a *soulmate connection*. The days of passionate sex and intimacy were long gone. The days of great communication and conversation had passed. However, the connection they had on a soul level lasted until the day Muriel passed. Robertson will tell you he had no regrets. Neither will you when you make the decision to root and ground your marriage in a soulmate connection. The first step to making the move from roommates to soulmates is to understand the essence of the soulmate relationship and to return to the promises you made the day you married. The second step is making the decision to create a phenomenal marriage by design.

Action Steps from Chapter 1

1. Discuss with your partner your understanding of soulmates prior to reading this chapter. How has this chapter helped you in your pivot from roommates to soulmates? Make the decision today to root and ground your marriage in a soulmate connection.
2. Find your wedding vows and print two copies. Give a copy to your spouse and schedule some time to talk about the promises. Think and talk about ways that you can make these promises more central to the DNA of your marriage. Go to www.FromRoommatesToSoulmates.org for a list of five more ways to make your vows part of the DNA of your marriage.
3. Go to YouTube and type in Robertson McQuilken Resignation Speech. Listen to the two-minute segment.

CHAPTER 2
Marriage By Design

DO YOU REMEMBER when you first applied for your driver's license? In the state where I grew up, acquiring your driver's license was a two-step process. The first part of the process included a written exam. The test was complete with questions about traffic laws, signage, stopping distances, and driving techniques. The only way to pass the test was to study, and in Pennsylvania many people did not pass the test on their first try. The second part of the process was the actual driver's test. Again, many people did not pass this test on their first go around. The state of Pennsylvania did not make it easy for 16-year-old kids to get their driver's license. Many 16-year-old kids had to take the test multiple times. The theory behind this difficult process was that for the rest of your life you would be driving a vehicle at high speeds, between two yellow lines, with other cars driving towards you, in all types of weather and road conditions. This is a big deal that required intentionality, training, and some expertise.

In the same way, your marriage is a big deal. You will be traveling together in situations that will constantly be changing, in all different seasons of life, with a great deal of surprises and life challenges that have the potential to rock your marriage. Many people reading this book already know that truth all too well. But, unlike the driver's license, all that is required to get married is a signature at the courthouse. The license to get married is far easier to acquire than a driver's license, but the damage that a failed marriage can cause rivals the worst car wreck. This is one of the reasons that I have written the book that you are now reading.

I wish I had a dollar for every person who has come into my office and said the words, "I wish I would have known these principles before I got married." The people who say this are good people who have made bad marital decisions and now they are fighting to save their marriages. Sometimes when I share these principles, they are brand new revelations to my clients. Those people simply had no idea.

Sometimes they did know of the principles, but they did not realize how important they were to creating a PHENOMENAL MARRIAGE that would last over time. The good news is that as these clients learned these principles and began to utilize them in their broken marriages, their marriages began to improve. These principles are the key to creating a phenomenal marriage. The exciting thing is that marriages begin to pivot rapidly when you begin to apply the principles that you will read about in this book. The challenge is that most couples build their marriages not by design, but by default or drift.

It's essential to build your marriages by design and *not* by default or drift.

I have been a Lutheran Pastor for over 30 years and during this time I have conducted over 200 weddings. Imagine if at those weddings I had approached the groom the day I was doing the wedding and asked them a question about the future of their marriage. Imagine me asking the groom the day of their wedding, "Paul, do you think you and Lisa are going to have an average marriage?"

How many of the 200 grooms would reply, "Yeh, I think we are going to have an average marriage."

Imagine if I had asked you the day you married, "Do you think you are going to have an average marriage?" How would you have replied? You would probably respond the same way the 200 grooms would. You would look at me and say, "Rispoli, you are an idiot. Why would you ask such a stupid question? No, we are not going to have an average marriage, we are going to have a phenomenal marriage!"

Most everyone who marries does so because they assume they will have a great marriage. No one gets married to have an average marriage. But here is the problem. Most of these couples do not have a clue on what a "great relationship" or "wonderful marriage" looks like. For many of them they have not even thought about having a phenomenal marriage.

Frequently I ask couples in my office, "Who do you know that has a great marriage?" I am always amazed and saddened at how difficult it is for people to answer this question. The second challenge is that most people use one of two strategies that do not work. They either use the "strategy of *drift*" or the "strategy of *default*."

*Are you using the **'drift strategy'** in your marriage?*

Most of the couples that come into my office utilize the strategy of drift. They got married and were deeply in love. They just assumed that everything was going to stay the same and that the physical and emotional connection would stay constant regardless of the changes in their social and life environments. If I had asked them the question the day they married, they would have told me that they were going to keep doing what they were doing and eventually they would just drift into this phenomenal marriage place. But we all know that when things are drifting, they never drift up and to the right. Things always drift downstream.

A marriage that is drifting will always drift downstream.

For many couples utilizing the *drift* strategy, they find that they have drifted apart and are far from their starting point the day they married. If you have no strategy at all, chances are you have been utilizing the *drift* strategy and did not even realize it.

*Or, are you testing out the **'default strategy'** in your marriage?*

The second strategy that people utilize is the strategy of *default*. The strategy of default happens when couples default to either what they have always done relationally or to what they have seen their parents do in their marriages. This is one of the reasons that the divorce rate for second marriages is higher than the divorce rate for first marriages.

The strategy of default never works. Unfortunately, many of us had parents who did not model the healthiest of marriages. Styles of relating, roles and rules of each partner, and communication styles may or may not serve our marriage well. But if this is all we know, and this is the way we were raised, we carry this into our own marriage.

Marriage by default is only allowing your marriage to rise to the level of the best marriage you have studied or observed.

Even when we are consciously aware the marriage did not work that great for our parents, we still find ourselves functioning like our parents. Even as a middle-aged man, I have frequently been surprised how often I behave like my own father. This includes the good, the bad, and the ugly.

Marriages by default will have the good, the bad, and the ugly of the marriages in their past. It's a fact...

- *You did not marry your mother.*
- *You did not marry your father.*
- *You did not marry your ex-spouse.*

The strategy of default never works.

Discover a Better Way for Your Marriage!

In this book, I am proposing a *better way* for marriages. This *better way* is a way that has created PHENOMENAL MARRIAGES for newly wedded couples, as well as restored marriages that have been broken by default or by drift. Yes, it's a *better way* that has generated hope for couples that have been on the brink of divorce and has given a vision and plan for couples who are just starting out. It is a *better way* that my wife and I have followed as we have enjoyed our *phenomenal* marriage.

The *better way* is...
MARRIAGE BY DESIGN

I call it **MARRIAGE BY DESIGN** because it starts with an intention to create and to have a phenomenal marriage. The dictionary defines the word *phenomenal* as "very remarkable, amazing, and extraordinary." I love the word "phenomenal" because it captures the essence of what we all want for our marriages when we decide to marry our spouse. There is something that is different about the one we choose to marry. He or she stands apart

from all the other potential suitors. We fully believe and are convinced it is possible to have a
> remarkable,
>> amazing,
>>> extraordinary marriage
>>>> yes, *phenomenal marriage.*

The good news is that *it is possible.*

The Good News is that it is possible to have a…
Marriage by Design

A **Marriage by Design** starts with the intention to build a *phenomenal* marriage. The number one key to creating a *phenomenal* marriage is to decide that you *will* create one.

One of my mentors, Anthony Robbins, has said, "It is in the moments of our decision that our destiny is shaped.[4]" Through the years, I have learned that our destiny is also impacted by the decisions that we have failed to make. Decide *today* that, regardless of where you are in the marital journey, you will create a remarkable, amazing, and extraordinary marriage.

A Marriage by Design Must Have a Proven Plan

So, your *better marriage* must be a **Marriage by Design** which has a **proven plan.** The proven plan outlined in this book is 100% GUARANTEED to create a *phenomenal* marriage. If you follow this plan, you will have a great marriage. Whether you are just starting out on your marital journey or have been married for a long time, the principles in this plan will work for you.

One thing that many people discover in following this plan is that it initially seems like there are a lot of moving pieces. You might find yourself saying, "How will I ever keep all of this straight?" or "How will I remember to do all of these things?"

Don't be discouraged. Remember when you were first learning how to drive? There were so many steps involved in making a U-Turn, so many things you had to be mindful of, and yet for most of us, this just comes second nature now. The same will be true as you follow the principles of marriage by design. Eventually these relationship habits will become second nature in the relationship.

You won't go on *drift* or *default*, but the habits will become part of the DNA of your marriage. When this happens, you will have a *phenomenal* marriage.

Get Ready to Get Clarity on What a *Phenomenal Marriage* Looks Like

In the next chapter, I will lead you through a process that will give you more *clarity* about what your phenomenal marriage will look like and a tool that you can use to make sure that you never stray from this ideal.

Regardless of where your relationship is today, this tool will help you identify a future that is incredible and begin to see that it really is possible. The next step in marriage by design is to understand how your belief systems have the potential to impact your marriage for greatness or keep your relationship stuck. Understanding how your mind and beliefs affect your relationship, as well as how you can change your beliefs, can be a catalyst to create not only a better marriage but a better life.

You will also understand and develop the habits that can create a phenomenal marriage. In these chapters, you will learn the habits that can create a phenomenal marriage. These are habits I have observed in the hundreds of phenomenal marriages that I have had the opportunity to work with throughout the years. The final step is understanding the importance of developing a plan to protect your marriage from the outside forces that pose the greatest threats to you and your spouse.

Did I mention that I failed my driver's test the first time I took it? I made the mistake of taking the driver's portion of the exam in the pouring down rain. I could not see the yellow lines on the driver's course, and at one point I was driving on the wrong side of the road. The next time I took the test, I took it on the most beautiful sunny day of the year. I have been driving for over three decades now, and I am so glad that I did not throw the towel in on this concept of driving because I initially failed.

Likewise, you may be relationally driving on the wrong side of the road and feel as if you have been failing in your marriage. Like the rain, there may have been outside factors that now have your marriage off track. **Don't give up.** There is hope.

You have already made the decision to root and ground your marriage in a soulmate connection. You have returned to the promises that you made the day you married. Now you have made the intention to create a *phenomenal* **Marriage by Design**.

Remember, a *phenomenal* marriage is a marriage that is remarkable, amazing, and extraordinary. Now, turn the page, and let's start to create your phenomenal marriage by design.

Action Steps from Chapter 2

1. Discuss with your partner, who in your life appears to have a *phenomenal* marriage? What makes you believe that their marriage is *phenomenal*?

2. Discuss with your partner what was your initial vision for your marriage and what was your initial strategy? How has this worked for you?
3. Make the decision today that you are going to create a phenomenal marriage by design. Go to www.FromRoommatesToSoulmates.org to download a free Phenomenal Marriage poster and screen saver.

CHAPTER 3

The Marriage Manifesto

ONCE UPON A time, children dreamed about growing up and getting married. They envisioned their wedding day. Believe it or not, many of these children would play dress up and conduct the ceremony in the back yard. It was magical and brilliant. For many of the children, the vision included a walk down the aisle where they would meet their prince or princess. This pretend session was complete with all the props. One person would play the officiant, there would be the wedding couple, the bridesmaids and groomsman, and even flower people. The two would say their wedding vows, have children, and live happily ever after.

Perhaps you played a similar back yard game when you were young. It reflected a day in our culture where kids could be kids and their biggest worry was to be home before dark. I miss those days. Children are no longer dressing up and conducting weddings in their back yards. I wish I could say that the reason for this is the sophistication of today's toys. It would be great if we could blame this phenomenon on social media, XBOX and the internet. Sadly, we all know this is not the cause of our children no longer playing the wedding game.

In a society where marriages have become replaceable and the divorce rate has become 50%+, I am not sure children believe happily ever after is possible. Divorce has impacted one of every two kids in our elementary schools. Many of these children have been through multiple divorces. If happily ever after is not possible, why should we even try? The truth is that many of our millennials are making the decision that perhaps marriage is not worth it. The current trend among millennials is to live together and hang out. If it works, that's great. But if it does not work, they can move on without the hassle of a legal marriage. After all, it did not work out so well for many of their parents.

In previous decades, children had a vision for marriage that would end in happily ever after. I believe that this vision served these children and their marriages well. The truth is that happily ever after marriages really are possible. In working with literally thousands of couples from around the world, I have learned that the happiest, most successful marriages are couples that not only believe this, but they also have a vision for what a phenomenal marriage would look like for their relationship. Not only do these couples have a vision, they have talked about it, and they have also developed a plan.

I want to assure you that a *phenomenal marriage is possible for YOU!*, but that possibility can only happen if you are able or equipped to identify what it would look like for you. Unfortunately, many of us have been indoctrinated with messages like there is no such thing as a great marriage. Marriages are often referred to as a "ball and chain." Spouses are even referred to as "my old lady" or "my old man." And these are words of endearment? How frightening is that! Is it any wonder that we have lost our vision for great marriages? Not only are we short on positive role models, many of us don't have a clue on where to start.

I have experienced two very successful marriages. In both cases, I was led through an exercise like the one that I am going to explain in this chapter before we got married. The first time was with Cathy; we had been dating for a year and three months and we were planning on getting married in nine months. We met with the minister who was going to conduct our ceremony. He led us through an exercise very similar to the one that I will share now.

After Cathy passed away, and I remarried, Jennifer and I were led through a similar exercise. It is the same exercise that I use in day long house calls all over the world. Couples will fly me to their home to spend 8 hours around their kitchen table. They always assume that I am going to begin the day by talking about the marital problems. I never do. I start with this marriage manifesto exercise. It deals with getting a vision for a phenomenal marriage. After all, no one gets married to have an average marriage. I believe we all want a *phenomenal* marriage.

A phenomenal marriage is a marriage that is remarkable, amazing, and extraordinary.

The Revelations of a Marriage Manifesto Will Help You

Great marriages don't just automatically happen. They happen when couples get a vision for what their great marriage is going to look like. Specifically, they get clarity about what is present and what is absent in their marriage. I call this the "marriage manifesto." Ideally, this should be done before you get married, but it is never too late to get clarity about what a great marriage would like for you.

The word *manifesto* traces its roots to the Latin *manifestum*, which means clear or conspicuous. A manifesto is defined as a declaration of one's beliefs, opinions, motives, and intentions. This document declares what is most important to a person or organization. A manifesto functions as both a statement of principles and a bold, sometimes rebellious, call to action. *When couples acknowledge the gap between their manifesto and their current reality, the manifesto can challenge assumptions, foster more commitment, and provoke change.*

1. **The first step in creating a *marriage manifesto* is to begin to dream again.** Give yourself permission to dream big. Regardless of where your relationship has been, your past does not have to equal your future. You have the freedom to begin to imagine a perfect marriage. Ask yourself,

    "If my marriage was absolutely *phenomenal*, what would it look like?

    "What would be present if my marriage was exactly the way I wanted?"

Then, *write these things down in a list*. Just let your imagination fly and write down everything that comes to your mind. You are developing a list of things that would be a part of your marriage if your marriage were *phenomenal*. For this first step, we are assuming great communication, respect, and quality time together are going to be present. Think about what else is present. This is your "A List."

For my wife and I, we came up with a list of ten things that were present. The first thing present was our *faith*. We share a similar faith background, and we knew from the start that our faith was going to be the cornerstone of our marital lives.

Secondly, next to each other, our *children* were the most important people in our lives, so we knew that our kids would be a significant part of our marriage. We both had a conviction that the relationship needs to be our number one priority above anything or anyone else. We like to have fun, have new experiences, and we are both huge Cardinal fans who love baseball.

Sex is important to us. We were not going to be in a sexless marriage.

We knew we wanted to do a lot of *traveling* with each other, with family, and with friends.

We knew we needed *financial* stability and *security*.

And, finally, we both are generous and agreed that a sense of contribution, volunteer, and giving would be important to us. We made this list and we said we wanted these things to be a part of our lives.

We developed a common list. Naturally, there were some items or ideas on my wife's list that were not on mine, and there were some things on my list that were not on hers. We discussed these issues and compromised, and some of the items or ideas were added to the list. Sometimes the ideas and items were not on our common list, and we couldn't add them to the manifesto. In that case, we had to say, "Ok, that is your thing, and it is alright as long as it does not interfere with our relationship".

For example, if my wife is passionate about jazz music and I am not, it does not imply that I must suck it up and become passionate about jazz, nor does it imply that she can't have this as part of her life. It is just not one of the core values of the relationship. Maybe I love golf and that is my thing, but not my wife's. It does not mean that I am not going to play golf. It just means that golf is my thing. The important thing is that you come up with a list of core values that lead and guide your marriage. Remember, it is a dream list of things you can agree on and are present for both of you when the relationship is *phenomenal*.

2. **Now beyond your List A, get clarity on your List B of INTOLERABLES.** So, List A includes the core values that you agree are important to each of you. Now for List B…

Next work on being clear and transparent clarity about the things you are not going to tolerate in your marriage relationship. These are usually the ghosts from past failed relationships or deeply engrained life patterns that for you and your spouse have potential to become damaging blocks.

List B includes those things that you don't want in the relationship. You can call these your intolerable behaviors. For my wife and I, we have three items on our B list. The first item on our B list was *emotional black outs and relational chills*. We made a commitment that there would be no room in our marriage for distance. The second thing on our B list was *negative talk*. We are both committed to being radically positive. Finally, *we would not tolerate lying or cheating*, as my wife's previous marriage was ended when her husband cheated on and subsequently divorced her.

Things we would NOT TOLERATE in our *phenomenal* marriage were:

- **Emotional blackouts & relational chills.**
- **Negative talk.**
- **Lying and cheating.**

This exercise of getting clarity about what you want in your relationship is critical for creating a great marriage. If you don't have a vision for what a phenomenal marriage looks like, how will you know that you have one?

Get clarity about what you want your marriage to look like. Make two lists. List A is the list of things that you want to be mutually present in the marriage. This is the list of things that you both agree are important to the two of you—core values. These are not necessarily the relationship habits, but these are the nuggets that make life rich and rewarding for the two of you. List B is the list of things that you have agreed will not be present—the intolerable. These are the things that, when present, weaken or break connection. Just getting clarity on these things will bring the two of you closer.

After you have reached a consensus about what is present and what is missing, draft a paragraph that paints a word picture of what is present. This document becomes the manifesto of the marriage. Read it frequently and talk about whether your life and your marriage are matching the statement. Here is an example from my own marriage:

> *God, faith, and church are life priorities for both of us and they play an integral role in our marriage. We are each other's highest priority over any other person or distraction. We always present a united front. Our children are extremely important to us and know that they are deeply loved and our highest priority next to our marriage. Physical touch is present on a daily basis, ranging from G to R. We travel frequently, nationally and internationally, long and short trips, with and without kids, friends and extended family.*
>
> *We have fun and look for new experiences on a regular basis. We work hard to create security and financial abundance so that we can play hard and give generously. We attend 20+ Cardinals games a year and travel the country visiting different stadiums. We connect with friends on a regular basis. There is no room in our relationship for emotional black outs, chills, negative talk, lying, or cheating. We have a conviction that our life is good and the best is yet to come."*

This statement gives us a great deal of clarity about who we are as a couple. We know that when we are living this way our marriage feels wonderful. We crafted this statement before we were married, and it has governed and guided our relationship significantly throughout the years.

If you want to have a *phenomenal* marriage, get clarity about what a great marriage looks like for you. Take these steps...

- Don't get hung up on the wording and know it is not going to be perfect. Continue to work with it and tweak it.
- Get a vision that can get you excited. This is only the first step, but it is important. Realize that the vision can change. Update it as frequently as you need to; the important thing is that you are talking about it.
- Talk about what is present and not present and put it in a statement. It can become a compass for the relationship.

I have done this exercise with couples on the brink of divorce, and it has inspired them to stay married and create their dream. Regardless of where things are for you right now in your relationship, commit to creating a marriage manifesto. If you are engaged, newly married, happily married, or your marriage is on the brink of divorce, this exercise is powerful and can be a game changer for your future. When you first do this exercise, you may discover that there is gap between the picture that you have painted and your current reality. In the next chapter, we are going to talk about the beliefs that will keep you stuck and the beliefs that will help you begin to move forward to create and live in this place that you have envisioned.

Action Steps from Chapter 3

1. Go to www.FromRoommatesToSoulmates.org to see more examples of other couples' Marriage Manifesto's.
2. Take the time to complete the Marriage Manifesto Exercise. Consider printing it out and putting it in your smart phones.
3. Make a habit of reading it together daily. Remember that what you focus on, you manifest.

CHAPTER 4
Belief Systems

THE NEXT KEY to having an absolutely *phenomenal* marriage is:

A *phenomenal* marriage is supported by the right mindset and beliefs.

Our brain is the hardware that operates our life. Truthfully, the quality of our lives greatly depends on this hardware. If you are not satisfied with the results you are achieving in any area of your life, chances are it is a hardware problem. Many of us need to upgrade the way we have been using our minds if we are to create a better future.

I have discovered there are certain beliefs that keep couples stuck in average, or even bad, marriages. One of my lifelong mentors has been Anthony Robbins. He says, "Once accepted, our beliefs become unquestioned commands to our nervous systems, and they have the power to expand or destroy the possibilities of our present and future."

Many couples really desire and have a vision for *phenomenal* marriage, but fail to adopt the belief system that supports a great marriage. Certain beliefs that a couple may adopt will certainly destroy the possibility of ever having *a phenomenal* marriage. However, other right beliefs can grow and expand a couple into a phenomenal future.

It's essential for a couple to eliminate limiting belief and adopt beliefs that will support a couple in their positive, relational goals. Whether you are just starting out your marital journey or already have a long history, tap into beliefs that support your future as opposed to limiting it.

Eliminate Limiting Beliefs

1. Eliminate the limiting belief that "**There's no such thing as a great, *phenomenal* marriage.**"

This belief is usually peppered with comments like, "marriage is hard" or "No one is perfect" or "It is as good as it can be." These kinds of statements generally keep the relationship stuck. Many of the people who cling to this belief have had poor relational models. Frequently, their parents did not model what a great marriage could look like. People who get trapped by this belief tend to hang out with people who don't have great marriages. Many of these individuals would be hard pressed to identify at least one great marriage. The challenge with this belief is...

> **If you don't believe your marriage can be *phenomenal*, you won't take the actions to make it great.**

It's helpful to seek out as mentors and friends, couples who are five to ten years older than you with great, healthy, positive marriages to learn from. Look up to and learn from marriages in which husbands and wives are deeply in love and are successfully doing life together. These *phenomenal* marriages are found in newly married couples, couples who have children, empty nesters, and couples who have never had children. Again, the problem is if you believe there is no such thing as a great marriage, how would you ever have one yourself? This limiting belief will keep you stuck in an average or below average marriage.

As a Lutheran Pastor, I have conducted over 200 weddings in the past 30 years. Not one of these couples came to me and said, "We want to have an average marriage." When we get married, we just assume the marriage is going to be great, but when things get hard, we surrender this belief and settle for average. So, ditch the limiting belief that there are no such thing as great marriages. Set your bar high and work hard to make it *phenomenal*.

2. The second limiting belief that destroys the possibility of a great marriage is **"My spouse will not or cannot change.**

This limiting believe is evidenced by people saying things like, "You can't teach an old dog new tricks" or "You can't take the stripes off of a zebra" or "Once a cheater, always a cheater." If people were dogs and zebras this belief might be true, but the reality is that every one of us has potential to change. Frequently the person who is holding onto this belief has experienced radical changes in their own lives. I say, "You have changed, why don't you think your spouse can change?" This belief tries to lock people into their past and define them by their behaviors.

People who want to and who have good counsel and guidance, can change, when they choose to change over pain.

When the pain of a bad marriage becomes greater than the fear of change people will reach out for help and seek positive ways to change. **People change all the time.**

- I have seen serial cheaters commit to their spouses,
- I've watched alcoholics get sober.
- I've observed people with anger issues become gentle non angry people, and
- I have counseled with controlling people who chose to surrender their need for control.

People really do change. You must believe that people can change. The limiting belief that people can't change will keep your relationship stuck and stymie your relationship's future.

3. The third limiting belief that destroys the possibility of a great marriage is **"Change always takes a long time."**

I often hear people say, "It took our marriage 20 years to get to this place, and we are not going to get on the other side of this for a very long time." When I hear this, I always reply, "If that is what you want you are probably right." We have been programed by psychotherapy and culture to believe that lasting change needs to take years. The truth is change can happen in an instant.

Change begins the moment someone makes a decision.

A huge, bestselling book by Katy Milkman, Ph.D. in behavioral psychology is "How to Change[5]." Here's some tips about how to change her award-winning research has discovered with my added comments:

1. *Positive change can happen when you decide to make a **fresh start**.*

2. ***Avoid impulsivity.*** *Trying to change long-term bad habits overnight is not the answer. Change of direction does bring immediate results. But change that creates new habits does take some time, commitment, and work.*
3. ***Stop procrastinating.*** *If you need to change, get started now.*
4. *Stop promising to change and start keeping your promises.*
5. ***A great hindrance to change is laziness.*** *Faith without works is dead. Change without work never sticks.*
6. ***A final hindrance to change is conformity…doing what the media and the masses say a good marriage is.*** *Truth be told, the media and masses really don't have a clue about what a phenomenal marriage looks like.*

Regardless of how long you have been struggling with whatever the issue is, the truth is change happens the moment you decide to make a fresh start and commit your life to a new direction. Don't buy into the limiting belief that it is going to take forever for your situation to get better. Don't procrastinate and get help or counseling if you need to do so. Change starts the moment of your decision and commitment to begin to move in a new direction.

Couples are always amazed at how quickly they fall back in love once they stop fighting and begin practicing healthy relational habits. The belief that it takes a long time to get the relationship on the right track or turned around is a limiting belief that does not serve your relationship well.

4. The fourth belief that destroys the possibility of a great marriage is believing: **I can't forgive**.

Forgiveness is a critical element in creating phenomenal marriages. There will never be a hope-filled, loving relationship if you cannot forgive the past. Forgiveness does not mean forgetting the past. Forgiveness does not mean continuing to function in a way that puts you in an abusive or less than tolerable relationship.

Forgiveness means that you will no longer allow the events of the past to rob you of your future.

Forgiveness is deciding to let go of the past. You no longer have the right to hold past mistakes against the person. Forgiveness means that you are no longer stuck in the past. Forgiveness empowers you to choose to form new habits and walk into a positive future.

If you believe that you cannot forgive, you won't. Unforgiveness is allowing the past to determine and destroy your future. You will wake up and discover that your past has robbed you of your future. The truth is everyone can forgive. You must believe that you can, and then, you will forgive...you will move on...you will *get over it!*

5. The fifth belief that destroys the possibility of a great marriage is: **I am a victim.** Victims will often tell me, "David, you don't know what she did to me. You don't know what he did to me. You have no idea where we have been." I say, "It does not matter. You are not a victim unless you choose to be."

Break out of the victim role, so that you can create a better future.

Like the forgiveness challenge, victimhood keeps you stuck in the past. If you are a victim, you are allowing your past to sink your future. The challenge with victims is that they are powerless and stuck. Victims always lose and never come out on top. Victims require special treatment and don't have the strength to build anything because they need all the attention on themselves.

While you may have been repeatedly wronged in the relationship, the belief that you are a victim will keep your marriage stuck. You are not a victim. You are a powerful person with tremendous power to change and become anything you want. It is time to shed victimhood and embrace a new, stronger you. The belief that you are a victim will impact every area of your life and will keep your relationship stuck.

6. The sixth belief that destroys the possibility of a great marriage is: **My past must equal my future.** This is evidenced by couples saying things like "This is the 20th time we have been through counseling" or "We do it for a little while, and then we go right back to where we were." The challenge with this belief is that it does not leave room for the possibility that this is going to be the last time you will ever deal with an issue. Even though in the past you have wrestled with issues, and you have not yet figured out the right combination to break through, don't quit trying.

The truth is your breakthrough might be just around the corner. Again, like so many of these limiting beliefs, don't let your past rob you of a better future. You really need to believe that the future can be different, and it can be better.

Decide to believe that your future can be different and better than your past.
It's your choice.

Your past does not equal your future and the best is always yet to come. Hold on, things are going to get better.

7. The seventh belief that destroys the possibility of a great marriage is: **If my spouse is not willing to try, then it is no use**. I hear individuals say all the time, "It is no use, my spouse is checked out, or my spouse has given up." I explain to them that even though their spouse is temporarily checked out, they can still turn their marriage around.

This statement is based on two realities. The first reality is that people change their minds every day all day. Frequently a spouse that is checked out, having an affair, etc., believes that the marriage can never change. These spouses believe their past is going to equal their future. When they think about the future, all they can see is the past.

When these spouses begin to see the changes in you, they begin to change.

It is like the butterfly effect. The butterfly effect deals with how a butterfly flapping its wings in Japan can have an impact on the tides in New Jersey. So, it is with the power of unconditional love. Your unconditional love really can draw your checked out spouse back into the relationship. It makes no difference how far gone they say they are- I have seen love win them back.

No greater force exists in the universe than the power of unconditional love, and it can draw your partner back into the relationship. If your spouse is not on board or not as committed as you are to have a phenomenal marriage, stay the course. Take the lead for this season in your marriage and continue to put love first.

3 Beliefs You Must Adopt

There are three beliefs that every couple and every individual should full heartedly subscribe to regardless of what phase of their marriage they are in.

1. The first belief that can make a tremendous difference is: **I deserve to be in a *phenomenal* marriage.** This is not just an average marriage, not just a good marriage, but a *phenomenal* marriage.

    If phenomenal marriages exist, and we have already determined that they do, don't you think you deserve one? You must certainly *believe* that you deserve one. When you believe that you deserve a *phenomenal* marriage, you stop sabotaging the relationship and you start to function differently in the relationship.

    You also make a commitment that you are going to be working towards this great relationship. Everything changes when you believe you deserve a *phenomenal* marriage. And... you do!

2. The second belief you must adopt is: **I have the power to make the relationship *phenomenal*.** I am not helpless.

    Regardless of what you have walked through, regardless of where the relationship has been, make the decision today that you have the power to make your relationship *phenomenal*. You really do have this power, and I want to encourage you to dig deep and tap into it.

3. The final belief you must adopt is: **My past does not have to define my future.** No matter how many false starts you have had in the past, no matter how bad your programming has been, no matter how many times

you have failed before, this time is going to be different. This time you are going to embrace a future that is filled with hope and love. After all, you deserve it!

Declare, "I know the best is yet to come for me." Now that you have created the marriage manifesto and identified beliefs that have the potential to keep you stuck, it is time to embrace the habits of highly effective and *phenomenal* marriages.

Action Steps from Chapter 4

1. Go to www.FromRoommatesToSoulmates.org to see the list of the 7 Beliefs that will keep your relationship stuck.
2. What have been some of the beliefs that you have historically held, that have not served your marriage well?
3. Which beliefs do you most resonate with today?
4. Make the decision to believe that your marriage can be *phenomenal*. Believe that you have the power to make it *phenomenal*. Believe that you will choose and commit to making your marriage *phenomenal*.

CHAPTER 5

Respect

RODNEY DANGERFIELD, A famous comedian, once lamented, "When I was a kid, I lost my parents at the beach. I asked a lifeguard to help me find them. He said, 'I don't know kid, there are so many places they could hide'- Boy I tell you, I get no **respect** around here!"

Rodney Dangerfield's tombstone reads, "Rodney Dangerfield -There goes the neighborhood." His album called 'No Respect" won a Grammy Award in 1980. Rodney Dangerfield became famous because of the catch phrase "I get no respect" and his hilarious monologues around the subject of respect.

The phrase "I get no respect around here" is one that I hear frequently in my office working with couples in crisis. While the topic is hilarious at the comedy club, the reality of not being respected in a marriage is incredibly painful and damaging to the relationship.

A definition of *RESPECT* is…

> "to look upon or see someone with honor'"
> "to highly value or prize someone'"
> "to esteem or affirm the self-worth of someone."

This next key to a *phenomenal* marriage is *Respect*, a word that has lost its power in today's generation. Not too long ago, a friend of mine shared that she was leaving the teaching profession. I was surprised; she had only been teaching for about ten years. When I questioned her, she revealed the level of disrespect had reached an all-time high in the schools. I assumed that she was talking about the students.

What she shared next surprised me, "It is not the students. I knew all along about the decline of disrespect from the students. Now what we are facing is the disrespect from the young teachers graduating from college." This is a sad commentary on our culture. I am certain many teachers reading this will agree. While this sad commentary on our young people is disturbing, it is even more alarming that the cause of this disrespect starts at home with parents and other relatives disrespecting one another.

Our young people are not seeing their mothers and fathers and their relatives honor, esteem, and value one another. What they do see is conflict, gossip, put downs, divorce, slander, libel, abuse, and even legal actions against fellow family members. As a society, we pay a great price for this reality. Our marriages have paid an even greater price.

What Is Respect?

Permit me to further expand on and explain what respect is. First, it is expressing honor and esteeming others with our words, emotions, and behavior. Respect is most often conveyed not just by words, but by our non-verbal communication like body language, facial expression, tone of voice, and physical behaviors like abuse.

Next, *respect* is defined as a feeling or understanding that someone is important and should be treated in an appropriate way. Respect is a particular way of thinking about or looking at someone. As a verb, it means to admire deeply. Respect in your marriage can be demonstrated as making your spouse your number one priority and making the decision to always put love first.

Respect is honor. The definition of honor is the respect given to one who is admired, prized, esteemed, and valued. Respect is demonstrated by honoring and admiring our spouse.

Dr. Eggerich is the author of an excellent book called "Love and Respect" that became a New York Times bestselling book[6]. The book explores the differences in genders in terms of the concept of respect. While I agree with much of what is in the book and have recommended that couples read it, one premise that I do not agree with is the premise that men need *respect*, while women need love. Eggerich states that a husband's love motivates his wife's *respect*, which further motivates his love. In my work with couples, I have found that women are equally desiring respect. The truth is husbands and wives need both love and respect.

> **"Never be disrespectful to each other. Respect your spouse's feelings and opinions, especially when yours are different."**
> -William F. Harley, Jr. in *His Need, Her Needs*[7]

There are two enemies to the type of respect that can make a relationship great.

Enemy #1: *Relationship Drifting.* The first enemy is allowing the marriage to fall into the drift setting. Before couples get married, most spouses assume that *respect* is always going to be one of the cornerstones of the relationship. For many couples, the relationship overflowed with mutual *respect* and admiration while they were dating. It simply happened naturally. *In many ways, it was this level of respect that facilitated the initial connection.*

When I hear stories about initial meetings, early dating years, and pre-engagement life, they are frequently stories that are rooted in respect. The challenge is that respect requires intentionality and consistency. When individuals get comfortable with the relationship, it can frequently be one of the first things that begins to take a back seat. *Little things that used to get noticed go unnoticed.* The things that used to happen naturally no longer happen.

When a person does not feel respected in marriage, the connection begins to wane. This causes anger and resentment. Apathy begins to grow.

I remember as a young person hearing the line in a song, "You don't bring me flowers anymore." The song was about a relationship that had lost its zest and fire. *When respect wanes in the relationship, the relationship loses its zest and fire.* The relationship starts moving from great to good and then to average. *Phenomenal* decreases to fine or just okay. Passion wanes and conversations turn from affirming to critical.

Enemy #2: *Respect is no longer a priority.* The second enemy to respect is that frequently our relationship role models have not made respect a priority. We may look at the relationships around us and say, "Well at least we are not that bad!" For many people, they have not seen examples of loving relationships that are rooted in *respect*. Many couples have not had conversations about the topic of respect in the relationship, and yet it truly is a cornerstone of phenomenal marriages.

When *respect* has not been modeled and we don't see it in the relationships around us it can be difficult to know how to demonstrate a high level of respect in our marriage. In my experience no one sets out to be disrespectful. It just happens naturally. This is the reason that that habit of respect needs to be intentional.

Make Your Spouse Your #1 Priority

The first step in developing a high level of respect in your marriage is to make your spouse the most important person in your life. Marriage implies that your spouse should be placed in this position of honor in your life. Your spouse needs to be more important than your friends, your parents, your siblings, and your children. Your spouse needs to be more important than your job, your stuff, and your hobbies. Making your spouse the highest priority is the starting point for respect. Make the decision that your spouse is going to be the most important person in your life, and you are going to let them know it on a regular basis. Remember, the key to respect is positioning your spouse as the most important person in your life and letting them know it on a regular basis.

There are small rituals you can do to keep your spouse in this #1 position. *The key is consistency and intentionality.* For example, Jennifer and I frequently find ourselves in social settings. Sometimes Jennifer will have arrived at the destination prior to me. When I arrive, I am frequently met by friends or associates before I see Jennifer. These friends may want to have a long conversation or engagement with me as soon as I arrive. I always make a bee line straight for Jennifer. I am not rude to others, I simply say, "I will be back, I want to say *Hi* to Jennifer."

Publicly notice and greet one another. Jennifer may be in the middle of a conversation when I arrive. She simply says, "Excuse me," stops what she is doing, stands up and gives me a hug, and we greet. We then go back to whatever it is that we were doing. This small exercise is a constant reminder to each other that there is no conversation and no other relationship that comes close to the relationship that we have with each other. It also lets other people see that we are deeply in love and are each other's number one priority. This small act of respect has been part of the rhythm of our relationship since the beginning.

If demonstrating respect and honor of your spouse publicly has not been a part of your relational DNA in the past, make a commitment to start engaging in these behavioral patterns.

The concept of greeting is not one that should merely be focused on outside your house when you are in front of other people. This should also carry over to inside your own home when no one is around. Take notice of one another. For example,

> **Whenever one of you are out and you arrive home, the spouse who is at home should stop what they are doing, stand up and greet the other spouse.**

We were taught in the military that you never talk to a superior ranked person from the sitting down position. You stand up as a sign of respect. The same principle can be very powerful in terms of your marriage. Stand up and greet your spouse. Let them know that you are glad that they are home. You would not believe the number of people who have sat in my office with this as their biggest complaint. They talk about coming home from work and getting the warmest greeting from the family pet as opposed to the people who are supposed to love them more than anyone else. Again, these are small signs that demonstrate respect and honor to your spouse. When you get into the habit of demonstrating this kind of *respect* for your partner, you truly begin to transform the relationship.

Always Act in Your Spouse's Best Interest

One of the elements that facilitates respect is having the belief that your partner is always acting in your best interest and with the relationship as their number one priority. Frequently when we second guess our spouse's motives, we get offended and angry.

> ### Second guessing our spouse's motives is disrespectful. Don't do it!

Refuse to be offended. If you don't understand why your spouse is acting or says something that seems hurtful, respectful ask *why* and then be quick to listen, slow to speak, and slow to anger. Think before you speak. Count to nine before saying something and be kind. Proverbial wisdom instructs,

> ### "A gentle answer deflects anger, but harsh words make tempers flare."[8]

It is hard to demonstrate respect from this angry or offended space. The natural inclination is to withhold respect. Make the commitment that you are going to demonstrate respect and honor regardless of what your spouse says or does. Deal with the issues that have caused the anger, but don't let your anger stand in the way of showing your respect. Anger and offense will damage your relationship and keep you stuck in a destructive place.

Because of *respect*, I can honestly tell you that there are not two human ears on planet earth that have ever heard me say anything unkind or disparaging about my wife. I refuse to talk poorly about her to anyone. I know that she refuses to speak poorly about me to anyone as well. One of the ways this is evidenced is that every time I meet one of her friends, they say, "David, it is so nice to meet you, I have heard such amazing things about you!"

Decide that you are only going to speak life over your spouse when talking about them in public and to other people. Because of *respect*, I never raise my voice, call names, or cuss at my wife. All these behaviors would demonstrate disrespect. If you have been doing these things, decide to stop immediately.

There are three keys that tend to keep *respect* alive in your marriage.

Key #1: Intentionality. The first is intentionality. Frequently, respect does not just happen. You have to be vigilant of it. Keep your eye on it, because when you get careless or take your eye off of it, it is really easy to fall into default mode. Default mode is when you are not making your relationship your number one priority. Focus on it! Be proactive with your respect. Never wait to be respected before you give respect.

Along these same lines, don't take your cues on respecting your partner based on how they are treating you. Respect is not *quid quo pro*; it is a decision you make to put your spouse as number one in your life. So don't treat them the way they are treating you. Instead, treat them the right way: with respect regardless of how you are being treated. I can't stress the importance of being intentional in terms of respect.

It's so easy to get lazy and go into a selfish mode that simply says, "Oh, they know. I don't have to do these things." This attitude is a recipe for disaster. Many of the other relational habits that are discussed in this book all have their roots in respect. It is the cornerstone for spending time together, great communication, date nights, and every other habit that is discussed. Get this part right, and the other habits begin to fall into place.

Key #2: Make direct, personal, uninterrupted communication your top priority in your time together. A second area that leads to conflict in terms of respect is the area of managing electronics in the relationship. This is a phenomenon of disrespect that has grown in the past ten years. The rise of rapid texting and cell phone usage can significantly undermine your marriage. I hear stories about spouses who are constantly texting their friends and their family when they are spending "quality" time with their spouse. Make a commitment that your meals are going to be places and times where electronics are prohibited. Decide that you are not going to let texting or your phone take priority over your spouse. Practice putting the phone down, not answering it when it rings, and having some electronic free zones.

Three places that should absolutely become electronic free zones in your marriage are the dinner table, the bed, and date night. These are three places where having a cell phone, iPad, or computer do not lead to connection. I frequently hear from spouses that they are disgusted because they feel like their partner's phone or iPad is more important than they are.

Key #3: Put the needs of your spouse above the demands of your children. The third area that leads to a breakdown of respect is when one partner makes the demands of their children or their parents more important than the wishes of their spouse. This issue is about boundaries and having habits that serve the relationship well.

> **While your children are always going to be important, and you have tremendous responsibilities in raising them, your spouse needs to be your greatest priority.**
>
> **By modeling and teaching this to your children, you position them to have phenomenal relationships in the future.**

The greatest gift you can give your children is to make the decision that you are going to stay married. One truism I like is, "One of the greatest gifts you give to your children is loving your spouse." While we need to always honor and *respect* our parents, our *parents* and *relatives* also need to see that our number one priority is our spouse. When we get these things right, *respect* flourishes.

When we get the *respect* habit right in the relationship, we are on our way to creating a phenomenal marriage. Make a commitment that you are going to exercise and demonstrate in small ways daily how much you respect your spouse. Rodney Dangerfield made a great living and became the greatest comedian of all time with his phrase, "I get no respect." While it is great comedy, it is detrimental to a *phenomenal* marriage.

Continual and Constant RESPECT helps keep your marriage PHENOMENAL!

Action Steps from Chapter 5

1. Discuss with your partner the current level of respect in your relationship. On a scale of 1 to 10, 10 being you have the most respectful relationship, 1 being the worst, what would you rate your current relationship?
2. Come up with three habits that you could adopt immediately that could improve the level of respect that exist in the relationship. Implement them immediately.
3. Go to www.FromRoommatesToSoulmates.org for 5 more ideas on how to increase the level of respect in your marriage.

CHAPTER 6

Communication

THE THREE MOST common complaints I hear in my marriage coaching office about relationships are,

- *"We don't communicate."*
- *"She does not listen to me."* and
- *"He does not talk."*

If I had a dollar for every time, I heard one of these comments, I would be a billionaire. One of the exercises I have couples do when they come in and see me on their first visit is to share what the major issues are that are creating a disconnect in the marriage. I have them imagine huge garbage cans stacked against my wall and let them know that each can represents one of their issues. Their job is to put labels on the garbage cans. I let them know that no one ever gets beat up in my office, so they must be kind to one another, but I have them simply state what they believe is at the root of the core issues. These three issues come up more frequently than not.

Effective communication needs to be intentional, planned, and implemented. One of the habits of highly successful relationships is the habit of effectively communicating on a regular basis. I call it "effectively" communicating because the term effective means producing the desired results. Our challenge is that while we are constantly communicating, we seldom take the time to think about *communication* itself. If you want to improve communication in your PHENOMENAL MARRIAGE, you must be intentional and then implement. In other words, make a right decision and then take action.

There are three components to long-term effective communication in relationships. Effective communication involves mastering a set of effective communication skills, being intentional about having different kinds of communications, and having regular built-in communication touch points.

- Learn effective *communication* skills.
- Be intentional and decide to use different kinds of *communication*.
- Establish and implement regular *communication* touch points.

Effective communication never just happens. Initially, it will seem like a lot of work. Some wrongly assert that great communication should simply happen. Effective communication never just happens. It requires constant work and intentionality. The upside of communicating well with your spouse far outweighs the work you will put into doing the work. Like many of the habits, initially it may feel unnatural and uncomfortable, but the more you practice these habits, the easier they become. Eventually they will simply be part of the rhythm of the relationship.

What is communication?

Communication is the exchange of thoughts, messages, or information. Communication involves both the sending and the receiving of messages. Work and effort are required by both the sender and the receiver. When the person who is sending the message is careless or unintentional, they risk communicating messages that are not true or messages that will be misinterpreted.

When the person who is receiving the message is unprepared or not in a place to receive the message, he or she risks missing or misinterpreting the message. The modes of communication can be varied, and they include speech, signals, writing, and non-verbal behaviors.

As much as 90% of all communication is non-verbal...

- *Facial expressions*
- *Body language and posture*
- *Tone of voice, pitch, loudness*
- *Eye contact or lack of it*
- *Clothing, uniforms, artifacts*
- *Appearance*
- *Gestures*
- *Personal space*
- *Environment where the communication happens*

The truth is we are almost always communicating...sending and receiving messages constantly. The challenge in our relationships is that when we are not being intentional, we end up communicating the wrong messages. Conversely, we sometimes receive messages that were not the intention of our spouse. This leads to conflict.

6 Enemies to Effective Communication

In working with couples, I have found that there are six major enemies to effective communication.

6 Major Enemies to Effective Communication

1. **Believing communication just happens spontaneously.** The first enemy to effective communication is the thought or belief that effective communication just happens. Frequently couples think just because they are deeply in love that they should be able to effectively communicate. The reality is that:

    ## Effective communication requires work.

2. **Thinking that if ineffective communication is happening, a couple is no longer in love.** The next reality is if you and your partner are not effectively communicating, this does not mean you are no longer in love. It simply means you are missing the mark in terms of your communication skills. The good news is that communication can really improve when you begin to work on it.

    ## Love motivates us to keep working together to experience effective communication in our relationship.

3. **Living a fast-paced life.** The next enemy to effective communication is the fast-paced tempo of many of our lives.

    ## Effective communication cannot be microwaved. It requires time.

    Want to feel deeply connected to your spouse? Slow down the pace of your life and focus on communication. I frequently do day-long sessions with couples. These are day long intensives where couples leave the day with a blueprint for creating a phenomenal future. They are extremely effective. One of the benefits of the day is that it requires spouses who are generally rushed and hurried *to slow down* and pursue a deeper level of communication. What is so amazing to me is that while couples don't always end up seeing eye to eye on the issues, the sense that they were heard and understood is incredibly healing. If you want to improve communication, you are going to have to slow down and listen to your spouse.

4. **Having a poor choice of words.** The fourth enemy to effective communication is poor use of words. There are certain words that incite and cause spouses to want to stop listening. For example, the words can't, always, and never, and phases that start with the words, *"You need to"* seldom lead to effective communication. These words and phrases are deeply connected to guilt and shame. Guilt and shame do nothing for communication. I would recommend that you eliminate these words from your vocabulary. They do not help in effective communication and tend to keep the relationship stuck.

Never start a conversation with, YOU need to...

5. **Failing to clearly articulate your needs.** The fourth enemy to effective communication is not clearly articulating your relational needs. This enemy usually manifests itself in phrases like, "Well they should just know" or "They should not have to be told" or "I have already told them." Frequently, the truth is that your spouse does not know and chances are they do not read minds. Set your spouse up for success by clearly articulating what you want and what you need. Sometimes you may need to

repeat yourself, but eventually and ultimately you have a higher chance of getting your relational needs met when you make your needs clear to your spouse.

Kindly ask for what you need.

6. **Misusing electronic media in communication.** The fifth and final enemy to effective communication is one that my parents' generation did not have to deal with. The fifth enemy to effective communication is the misuse of electronic media in communicating. The excessive number of couples that have primary conversations via texting is both maddening and sad to me. Communication involves both sending and receiving messages. Frequently messages that are intended one way get misread and misinterpreted by the receiver.

Texting is the lowest form of communication and can lead to misunderstandings and conflict.

Never have conversations that should be done face to face via texting. Save texting for your friends, and people you could care less about, but when it comes to communication with the most important person in your life, have face to face, real time communication.

Work on overcoming these enemies to your communication with your spouse. Take baby steps but begin to get very intentional about how you move forward. I have found that overcoming these five enemies will lead to a greater level of communication and greater marital satisfaction.

Essential Keys to Effective Communication

1. **Develop the habit of being a good listener.** To be a good listener you have to become intentional. Effective listening means that not only have you taken the time to listen to the words that your spouse is saying, but you also understand the emotion and intent behind the words. To achieve this, you need to slow down, clear yourself of distractions, and focus. A challenge that spouses frequently has is being distracted by something else when their spouse is trying to communicate.

It's hurtful to multi-task when trying to communicate directly with one another.

One of the challenges spouses have is that they frequently want to multi-task when their spouses are communicating with them. This leads to bruised feelings, misunderstandings, and their spouses feeling like what was being said is not important. This is especially true when the topic being covered is one of the relational hot topics. Relational hot topics include conversations about money, the children, housework, and work.

One of the attitudes that is helpful in developing the skill of being a great listener is the attitude: *Value what your spouse is communicating.* There are times when we intentionally block out messages because we could care less about the deliverer. This is certainly the case when it comes to much of the advertising in our lives. There are so many products that we care less about that we simply make the decision to ignore the communication. We block it out. Unfortunately, we sometimes do this with the people we love. You have heard people say, "Oh, he has selective listening skills" or "He only hears what he wants to". While these phrases are usually intended to be derogatory, there is sometimes an element of truth to them.

✐ **2. Share what you are thinking and feeling.** Others cannot read your mind! The next key to effective communication deals with delivering messages. One of the areas that gets many couples in trouble is the expectation that your spouse can read your mind. Sometimes people say, "Well they should just know," or "How could they not know?" The truth is we frequently don't know, and this is more of a commentary on our ineffective communication rather than a sense of not caring.

✐ **3. Use the type of conversation that effectively fits the immediate situation.**

There are three types of conversations phenomenal relationships have on a regular basis. The term *conversation* comes from a Latin word that means, "to turn together" or "to change together." It implies the frequent coming together and the addressing of issues. Relationships that are phenomenal have a healthy blend of three very distinct types of conversation.

Logical Conversations. The first type of conversation is what is called logistical conversations. These are conversations that must occur to run the household. These conversations revolve around children, money, housework, employment, scheduling, and the day-to-day operations of running a household. Unfortunately, for many couples this is the only type of conversation that occurs in the relationship.

When couples complain they are living more like roommates than soul mates, this is usually one of the culprits. Frequently the tone of these conversations can be negative, especially when there are competing expectations about how things "should be."

Friendship conversations. The second type of conversation is what is called the friendship conversations. These are conversations that build the relationship like conversations about your day, what makes you happy, and what you are most excited about or looking forward too. These are dialogues where you share yourself and you learn about your partner. A friendship conversation can be fun and light. These are the conversations couples have at the beginning of the relationship that lead to connection and the "falling in love" feeling. One of the dangers in marriage is when partners only have these conversations with people outside of the marriage.

Love conversations. The third type of conversation is the love connection conversation. The purpose of the love connection conversation is for a spouse to deliver a message to their spouse that lets them know they are important to you, that you value the relationship, and that you genuinely care about them. This type of conversation is when you call in the middle of the day just because you were thinking about your spouse. It is a daily conversation where you deliver a message that says, "I adore you!" or "I can't wait to see you tonight". If you want to have a phenomenal relationship, you really need to have all three types of conversations.

- **4. Set up communication posts.** The final element to creating effective communication in a PHENOMENAL MARRIAGE is to have built-in communication posts for being certain that major issues are being addressed. These communication posts should be scheduled daily, weekly, and quarterly.

The daily communication post should be a time during the day that is set aside for intentional communication. It could be at dinner, right before bedtime, or first thing in the morning. The purpose of this communication post is to avoid the ships passing in the middle of the ocean feeling that couples frequently experience when they are not intentionally communicating.

The weekly communication post is for the purpose of high-level communication regarding issues and the running of the household. During this meeting, couples are encouraged to talk about the relationship, the issues, what is working, and what is not working. I recommend you have this meeting on the same day every week. The purpose of this meeting is to assess the relationship and the business of jointly running a home and managing life. This meeting should never last more than an hour and should only be postponed if both spouses agree.

Start the meeting by asking the question, "What are the best three things that have happened in our life this past week?" This serves as the highlight reel for the week. Then ask, "What is the one thing that did not work out so well this past week? What did we learn and how can we handle this situation better the next time it arises? What do we need to move on from this situation?"

The second set of questions include discussing: *what is working, what is not working, and what is the source behind what is not working?* This weekly relational business meeting exists to clear the air, to unclog missed communications, to fix and tune up. You have it on a weekly basis because the pace of life can be so quick that couples fail to communicate about big issues.

The key is for you to decide on the front end that you are not going to fight during this meeting. This meeting will not always be a feel-good experience, but it will help significantly with communication. It is called the weekly business meeting.

These communication ideas and concepts will help you create a PHENOMENAL MARRIAGE. Stay the course and don't give up. If one spouse is a little less motivated to communicate at this level, stay the course, stay patient, and keep trying. At first it may feel like a lot of work, but eventually it will be part of the rhythm of the relationship that leads to a PHENOMENAL MARRIAGE.

Action Steps from Chapter 6

1. Discuss with your partner the 5 enemies to effective communication. Which ones have you struggled with in your relationship and make some commitments to overcome these obstacles.
2. Go to www.FromRoommatesToSoulmates.org to download a list of 36 random questions that researchers from the University of New York developed to help strangers connect. Begin to use these in your friendship building conversations.
3. Set a date and time for your weekly business meeting.

CHAPTER 7

Date Night, Hobbies & Volunteering: The Trifecta of Togetherness

WHAT DO DATE night, hobbies and volunteering all have in common? They all provide tremendous opportunities for you to connect with your spouse. PHENOMENAL MARRIAGES are intentional in their pursuit of all three of these in terms of building a great marriage. I have found through the years that the very best marriages have all three of these connecting elements present. Usually, the couples who are in crisis and in my office are not doing any of these things together.

I ask them, "Are you going on a weekly date night?" *No!*

"Are you regularly engaging in a hobby together that you both enjoy?" *No!* "Are you regularly coming together to volunteer in the world and contribute to something bigger than yourselves?" *No!*

"Do you have a great marriage?" *No!*

The other side of this coin is that in all the years of working with couples, I have never once met a couple who did all three of these things and did not have a great marriage. Date nights, hobbies, and volunteering are the trifecta of togetherness. If you want to have a phenomenal marriage, design it so that you have elements of all three.

Date nights. In the beginning of most relationships, date nights come very easy. One of the things I love to do with couples is have them describe the beginning of their relationship. Whenever I ask couples about the early stages of their relationship, they almost always describe their early dates. I can honestly say that I don't remember one relationship where a person told me that they did not start the relationship with dating. I realize that in some countries where marriages are arranged, the dating process may be shorter; but even with arranged marriages there is an element of dating.

Dating is the bedrock of relationship formation. It is the concept of going out, having fun, connecting, and spending time together. Unfortunately for many couples, they stop dating right after the wedding. I am always amazed at the number of people who tell me they cannot remember the last time they went out on a date with their spouse. They use excuses like we don't have enough money, we are too tired, we don't have anyone to keep the kids, or we don't have anything to do. These excuses will be the demise of your relationship. PHENOMENAL MARRIAGES make dating part of the DNA of the relationship.

Whether you are just starting out on your marital journey, have been married for a long time, or your marriage is in a crisis, dating can be the catalyst to create a phenomenal marriage. Try doing a date night challenge for the next ninety days. Make a commitment that you are going to make dating your spouse one of your highest priorities for the next ninety days. Here are some general guidelines for date night.

1. First, you must leave the house. People try to tell me all the time, "We just stay home and watch TV for our dates". This is not dating; this is watching TV with your spouse. A date requires you to get dressed up for your spouse and leave your home. It is different than just staying at home.
2. Secondly, plan for the date to last at least two hours. This is two hours outside of the home where the focus is going to be on each other.
3. Thirdly, make a commitment to leave the electronics at home. This means no phones, no computers, no Facebook, nothing that would

distract you from making your spouse your sole focus of attention. The only electronics that should be present on date night are the electronics that provide a connection to the kids. In the car on the way to date night, stay off your phones.
4. The final rule about date night is that you are not to bring anyone along on date night. Date night is not friend night. It is not date night if you are hanging out with your friends. Date night is just for the two of you.

The date night challenge is to go on 12 dates in 12 consecutive weeks. During the date night challenge, try not to repeat the same date in a 12-week cycle. This means that you can only do a movie and dinner as your date night once. Take turns planning the dates. You will be amazed at the level of connection you will feel after a few weeks. I have been amazed at the power of date nights to save broken relationships. The simplest and most powerful piece of marriage advice I give to newlyweds is to make dating once a week a high priority.

Mutual Hobbies

The second opportunity for togetherness is engaging in mutual hobbies. A hobby is a regular activity done for enjoyment, typically during leisure time. Hobbies can include collecting themed items and objects, engaging in creative and artistic pursuits, playing or watching sports, or pursuing other amusements. Finding time to invest in your relationship beyond work, home responsibilities, and children can be very hard. I can hear someone saying, "Wait a minute. We are already going on a date once a week, why do we have to pursue a mutual hobby?" You pursue a mutual hobby because you don't want to end up in the place that so many couples do, where they say they have no common interest and nothing in common. Jennifer and I have several hobbies that we pursue together. Our passion is the St. Louis Cardinals and professional baseball in general. We really enjoy going to games, talking about games, bringing friends to the games, and everything baseball. One of our goals is to make it to every major league baseball stadium. Another one of our hobbies is our saltwater aquarium. This has provided hours of entertainment watching our water friends. It is an expensive hobby, but it is something we really enjoy doing together. A third hobby that we have is comedy. We enjoy visiting comedy clubs. The laughter is great for our marriage, and we have enjoyed so many great shows. Identify hobbies that you can embrace and enjoy. Try them together and if does not work out, pick another one. The key is that you are pursuing activities you do together for fun. The way to make this successful is to make it a priority. Make spending this time together a priority for the relationship. Lastly, having mutual hobbies does not mean you are not going to have your individual hobbies. You will still have his and her hobbies. This does not mean you spend every moment together. It simply means you have at least one mutual hobby.

Volunteer Opportunities

The final opportunity for spending time together is volunteering together. One of the fastest routes from going from to me to we is to invest your life into something that is bigger than yourself. Sadly, many people only do things that will benefit themselves. Maybe these people were never taught about the value of making a difference in the world. Maybe these people have a fear that if they give to others, they are not going to have enough time for themselves. Maybe they feel like they don't have enough time to give to others. Maybe they are just selfish. But a life lived only for self is a small life. High schools all around the United States have discovered this truth, evidenced by an element of community service as a requirement of many high school graduations. Young people are taught the power of giving yourself, your time, and your resources to make a difference. Couples who have phenomenal marriages have also figured out the importance of contribution.

There are three reasons contribution is so important for your relationship. The first reason is that contribution gives your relationship a heightened level of purpose. For Jennifer and I, our sense of contribution comes from our church. We love being involved. We love giving our time and money. And we especially love doing it together. We know that together we are making a difference. A large part of our non-working time is spent serving and leading in our local church.

The second reason contribution is so important is that it gives us the opportunity to do something significant together. Unlike hobbies that may or may not be gender specific, serving and volunteering is not a respecter of genders. Everybody can do it. Getting involved in a service project can give you the opportunity to build teamwork in your relationship. Getting involved in a service project can give you common ground to talk about, to celebrate, to give your time to. Long after you are done volunteering and serving, your relationship will bear the fruits of having done it together. This sense of making a difference really does elevate an average relationship to a phenomenal relationship.

The third reason contribution is so important in your marriage is that it provides an opportunity for you to model to your children and to others that life is about making a difference. Your kids are watching you. If you are selfish and self-absorbed, your kids will be selfish and self-absorbed. If you are giving and loving, your kids will be giving and loving. Getting involved in a project is an opportunity for your kids to jump in and help you. It gives your family something to center around.

The final reason contribution is so important is that it feels good to know you are making a difference. When you give, your own heart gets bigger. One of the reasons so many people have such small hearts is that they have never exercised their giving muscle. We were not created just to be a sponge, where we just take, take, take. After a while, we become over saturated and are good for nothing. A life that is spent giving to others is a life well spent. The benefits of working together on something bigger than yourself, bigger than your problems, bigger than your relationship, and giving yourself to something that will last beyond you is a worthy endeavor.

Here are some guidelines on picking your volunteer opportunities. The first way to pick something to get involved in is to identify what you are most passionate about. Sit down and have a conversation about what gets your blood pumping. What has the potential to keep you up at night? What do you feel strongly about? Ask your spouse what are you most passionate about? Passion represents that thing that can keep you up talking all night. Some people will say they are not passionate about anything. They are not lying. Their passion button is broken. But the good news is that the passion button can get revitalized by simply beginning to do something. Here are some possibilities: Habitat for Humanity, working in a soup kitchen, tutoring kids after school, going on foreign mission trips, cancer awareness walks, church, politics, or volunteering at the Humane Society. Secondly, decide how much time you realistically have to give to the project. Mutually agree upon how much time you can devote to this endeavor and how frequently you will serve together. If you are new to volunteering, quarterly is a great place to start. Make a commitment to spend 4 days a year volunteering in a soup kitchen, working on a home for habitat for humanity, or serving at the nursing home.

Phenomenal marriages happen when couples intentionally look for opportunities to spend time together. Dating, hobbies, and volunteering are what I call the trifecta of togetherness. Design your relationship to have all three of these elements. You will be glad that you did, you will have a great marriage, and you will make the world a better place.

Action Steps from Chapter 7

1. Go to www.FromRoommatesToSoulmates.org to see a list of 25 possible date night ideas.
2. Go to www.FromRoommatesToSoulmates.org to see a list of 25 possible hobbies that you can do together.
3. Go to www.FromRoommatesToSoulmates.org to see a list of 10 possible volunteer opportunities.

CHAPTER 8
Touch & Sexual Intimacy

JENNIFER AND I love to go to baseball games. She is one of the greatest all around sports fans I have ever met; so, one of our favorite things to do is watch baseball. We have set a goal to visit all thirty professional baseball stadiums. Last year we made it to four different stadiums. All of them were awesome! They all featured great baseball, great people, and great food. One of the favorite parts of the experience for me has nothing to do with baseball and nothing to do with anything that happens on the field. It is the phenomena that occurs in every stadium around the fifth inning of the game—the kiss cam.

It is fun to watch people on the jumbo screen of the stadium as the camera hits them, and they are called to be "on." Sometimes, the unsuspecting couple never realize they are the ones being featured on the screen. Other times, the couple being shown is not really a couple or they are sitting next to someone who is not their spouse. I like it when the couple puts on a real show for the crowd and camera.

My favorite kiss cam shot is when there is a couple that are clearly in their senior years. These are the white-haired individuals that have lived more life than most of us who turn to their spouses and give the most wonderful embraces and kisses to each other. It always creates a cheer from the crowd. The message is that these old timers still have it. One of the marks of a PHENOMENAL MARRIAGE is the ability to touch and be intimate in a way that says, "We still have it."

Great relationships have touching and sexual intimacy as part of the rhythm of the relationship. Sex is not something that happens occasionally, or on special occasions. Sex is part of the fabric of the relationship.

We live in a society where there is a lot of sex talk and sexual images all around us. The marketplace has learned that sex sells. Sex is a multi-billion-dollar industry in the US. But I find when I am working with couples that, even though we are surrounded by sexual images and messages, we are not talking about sex with our spouses, and we are not having sex with our spouses.

In the 1970s, the term "Failure to Thrive" was coined. It came from a study where scientist discovered that children who did not experience a great deal of touch when they were babies developed a condition called failure to thrive. These touch deprived babies did not grow at the same rate as the other children. I would say that many relationships are experiencing the condition of "Failure to Thrive."

The Power and Importance of Touch

There have been many studies conducted on the power of touch. A study I read recently in the Wall Street Journal dealt with the power of touch in the hospitality industry. They conducted an experiment with waiters and waitresses. They wanted to find out if there was a correlation between the touch of the server and the amount of the tip. The results were astounding.

They found that when the server simply touched the hand or the shoulder of the customer when dropping off the bill, they received significantly higher tips than when they did not touch the hand or shoulder of the customer. It' true... touch leads to connection. Get into the rhythm of touching on a regular basis.

One place you can begin the good habit of touching is holding hands. Holding hands is a powerful statement to your spouse that you love them, you are desiring to touch them, and they matter. Another incredible upside to holding hands is that it sends powerful message to those around you that the relationship matters. When people see you holding hands, they will think you are a new couple, or you have just returned from a marriage enrichment program. Make it a habit to hold hands on a regular basis.

Next establish touch is in your everyday routine of doing life together. Whenever you have the opportunity, reach out and touch your spouse, on the face, on the arm, and the leg. Remember it does not need to be a sexual touch; it simply needs to be a touch that conveys you love them, and they matter. When you touch your spouse, think, "I am touching you because you really do matter to me. I am touching you because I adore you." Let touch be part of the rhythm of your life.

A common cause of marital discord is the lack of sexual intimacy. It is a theme that plays out in many relationships and can be a tremendous source of frustration and marital strife. *Newsweek* reports that 25% of couples have sex less than 10 times a year. Many couples desperately want it to be better but simply don't know how or where to start. Some of my clients complain that all their partner wants is sex and they are too tired, too angry, and not in the mood. Other clients complain that their partner is never available sexually and they are constantly being rejected. For others, sex is an elephant in the room as they go weeks, months, and sometimes years with no sexual intimacy.

The truth is, when you have a great marriage, you really do have great sex. If you want it to be better but don't know where to start, here are three going forward strategies that might be helpful.

1) **Communicate about sex.** Many of us grew up in homes where sex was never talked about, and the topic was laced with secrecy and shame. Subsequently, many adults are uninformed and uneducated about the human body, sexual intimacy, orgasms, and what it takes to please and satisfy their partner. This leads to silence and sometimes, when conversations do occur, they are conversations that are laced with guilt and shame. If you want your sexual relationship to be better, make a commitment to talk about it.

Talk about frequency and about what is working and what is not working. Talk about how your sex life could be better.

Try to identify the barriers and begin to eliminate them. For example, one of my clients recently shared with her husband that at the end of the day she was too exhausted for intimacy.

She asked him if once a week he would be willing to lessen her load by bathing the kids and cleaning the kitchen. As a result, she would be rested and willing to have more sex. He agreed and took it a step further by cooking dinner once a week and giving her one night a week where she was technically "off" from having to worry about anything. Their sex life has improved radically, and it has definitely improved their marriage.

I have another client who is in his mid-50s who shared he has been having problems sustaining an erection during sexual intimacy with his wife. The problem is that when this happens, his wife gets angry. Sometimes she accuses him of being unfaithful to her. She says the reason he is having erection problems is that he is getting sex elsewhere. When she is not accusing him of getting sex elsewhere, she believes the reason he is having difficulties is because he is no longer attracted to her. She believes he does not want to be intimate with her. What is the truth?

He is in his 50s and men in their 50s statistically begin to have challenges with erection. There is a reason that Viagra, Cialis, and Levitra are billion-dollar industries. This conflict could be solved by a very open and honest conversation about biology and a trip to the doctor. The important thing is that the two of you are talking about sex.

2) **Prioritize sex.** Make sexual intimacy a priority in the relationship. One of the strategies I share with many of the couples I work with is to schedule a weekly sex date. Schedule it. The rules of a sex date are you schedule two hours, foreplay is included, and you be creative.

A weekly sex date might initially feel contrived or mechanical, but it is better to schedule a weekly sex date and have sex 52 times a year than to have sex 6 times a year.

Scheduling sex? Really? Many couples do it, and it works for them. There is no rule saying this is the only time you can have sex, but it is one sure thing on a weekly basis.

3) **Realize that sexual connection starts outside of the bedroom.** Many of the women I work with complain that they feel as if their husbands neglect them all day long, and then they go to bed and want sex. I recall a client sharing recently, "He treats me poorly all day long, and then

we go to bed and he wonders why I don't want to have sex with him." Remember that sexual connection must start in the kitchen first thing in the morning. You can't expect to treat your spouse poorly and then for them to want to be intimate at the end of the day.

Respect, honor, putting your spouse first, communication, warm touch, giving, etc....all play into great sexual intimacy. Make the decision today that you are going to honor your spouse from morning till evening every day, and you will be amazed at how your evenings start to sizzle.

Three Enemies of Touch and Sexual Intimacy

The fast pace of our lives. There are three enemies to touch and sexual intimacy. The first enemy is the fast-paced speed of our lives. It is very difficult to get a touch connection and have sexual intimacy when one or both of you are traveling at the speed of light. I work with so many couples who are absolutely exhausted by the end of the day. The last thing on their minds late in the day is sexual intimacy. I have talked to many stay at home moms who report, "I have had kids hanging on me all day long, the last thing I want or need is my husband hanging on me in bed. I just want to sleep."

Many times, the couples I work with say they are too tired for intimacy at the end of the day. One of the strategies to mitigate this is to make plans on being sexually intimate at other times of the day. Sex does not have to just happen at the end of the day. Get into the rhythm of having sex at the times of the day where you both want to be intimate.

Children sleeping with you. The second enemy to touch and sexual intimacy is children or other people living with you. If you have small children sleeping in your bed, you are hurting your marriage and your kids. Many parents say, "Well this is just a stage and my child will grow out of it." I am sure your children will naturally grow out of this season. After all, who has ever heard of a 17-year-old wanting to sleep in their parents' bed? But it is not necessarily a healthy phase. Your children will go through many phases, but not all phases are equally healthy, and this one is potentially damaging to your child and to your marriage.

Your children need to learn that your bed belongs to you and your spouse. It is sacred. They need to sleep in their own bed, because your bed is only for you and your spouse. Your child may cry and get upset initially, but the lesson you are ultimately teaching your children is that your marriage and relationship with your spouse is your number one priority.

You may think you are meeting your children's needs in allowing them to sleep in your bed, but frequently I find it is really meeting the needs of one of the parents. Maybe it is the need to avoid conflict with their child. Or perhaps, it is the need to avoid intimacy with their spouse. Regardless, it is not healthy. You set your spouse up to be the bad guy and villain if you don't start to function differently. It is time to say, "Starting tonight, you must sleep in your own bed." When they do come into your room, take turns taking them back to their own room.

Pornography. The final enemy to touch and sexual intimacy is the pandemic of pornography. I call it a pandemic because it is a billion-dollar industry in the United States. Statistically, one out of every four men in the United States is hooked on porn. While there are many health risks associated to pornography addiction, the main challenge with porn is that it delivers a cheap and artificial substitute for connection and intimacy. The truth is it is a counterfeit. It is not real. I talk to guys who tell me it is just so much easier. While it may be easier, it is not right. Get set free from this and any other addiction that keeps you from touch and intimacy.

While you may never find yourself on a jumbotron at a major league baseball stadium, your marriage is a platform that is far bigger and far more important. Make touch and sexual intimacy part of the DNA of your marriage by design. Your spouse will know how much you love them and people will say, "They still have it.".

Action Steps from Chapter 8

1. Make a commitment to have a conversation with your spouse about sexual intimacy. Ask three questions. How satisfied are you with the frequency of sex in our marriage? How satisfied are you with the variety in which we engage in intimacy? What can I do to make sex better for you?
2. Go to the site www.Roommatestosoulmates.org for a list of 100 intimacy questions that you can use to start conversations and learn about your spouse's preferences.
3. Experiment with the sex date. Try it one time. I Dare You.

CHAPTER 9
Giving Presents and Presence

WHILE THIS CHAPTER on giving presents and presence may be one of the shortest chapters in the book, nonetheless, it is one of the best researched and foolproof ways to create a phenomenal marriage. In fact, I have never worked with anyone in marriage counseling whose marriage was in a crisis who were doing what I am going to ask you to do in this chapter. It is the one thing that is always absent in marriages that are not phenomenal.

Couples who are present and give presents do thrive. Couples who do not do this will eventually be in crisis. The chapter is short because the concept is so incredibly simple. PHENOMENAL MARRIAGES are marriages where couples give gifts of presents and are present to one another. It is that simple. Give your spouse a gift once a week. The power is not so much in the gift as it is the message behind the gift. This strategy even works for marriages in crisis.

Also, consistently give your spouse the gift of presence on a regular basis. The gift of presence is the message that you want to be with them, you enjoy hanging out with them, and you want to spend time with them. When these two gifts are present in a marriage, the marriage thrives. When one or both gifts are absent, the marriage does not thrive.

I am always amazed at the number of marriages that reserve giving gifts for birthdays and Christmas. Sometimes these average marriages give on Valentine's Day and anniversaries as well. A great deal of the marriages I work with have stopped giving on any of these days. These couples simply stopped giving to each other. No gifts, no cards, no flowers, no love notes, and no expressions of love. These couples give a list of excuses. "We mutually decided that we were not going to exchange gifts" is the most common. Other excuses I frequently hear are as follows:

- "It is a hallmark conspiracy."
- "I don't have to give to show that I love."
- "My spouse does not like to receive gifts."
- "We don't have any money.
- "I don't know what I would give to them."
- "It is not my or his/her love language."

So, for all these reasons and more, people don't give. Have you ever used one of these excuses not to give to your spouse? Chances are you learned from your parents' marriage what was appropriate or not appropriate in terms of giving.

The biggest excuse couple give for not giving gifts weekly is: *I don't know what to give.* **Really?! Forgive me but that's lame!** When I hear this excuse, I challenge them to begin to observe their spouse differently. I challenge them to begin to look for "gift opportunities" every day. The beautiful thing about this is that it requires your presence and beginning to know your spouse differently. Discover answers to these questions...

- What makes them tick?
- What is important to them?
- What are their hobbies?
- What are they worried about?
- What are they excited about?

- What are their favorite things?
- What keeps them up at night?

These questions can serve as a springboard for great gifts that have the potential to touch your spouse's heart.

Love is a verb not just a noun.

If love isn't only a feeling, what is it? Once the honeymoon wears off, love is primarily a verb, and to love someone is an active experience.

One of the challenges for us in terms of giving is that the concept has lost its connection to the concept of love. For many of us love is a noun. It is something that has landed upon us. I liken it to an exotic bird that mysteriously lands on couples. One morning they wake up and the bird has landed and now they are deeply in love. The challenge with this concept of love is that one morning they may wake up and find that the bird has left. This mysterious bird comes and goes, and when it is gone, we say we are no longer in love.

The truth is: *love is a verb. Love acts.* As Alanis Morissette said in a brilliant interview with Piers Morgan, "Love, to me, is a verb. Love kicks in for real when things get hard... Love, for me, is when I don't feel very loving. It's an action."[9]

Love in action involves giving and receiving gifts. In his book, *The Five Love Languages,* Gary Chatman has identified "gift giving" and "quality time" as two essential love languages[10]. (The other three love languages are "acts of service, affirming words, and physical touch.") You give because when you got married, you promised you would give to each other. Giving is one way that you can go inbound on a weekly basis with your spouse, physically demonstrating on a weekly basis that you are thinking about your spouse, and they matter to you. When you give to your spouse...

- you are demonstrating that they *matter to you, you care about them, you are thinking about them, and they are on your "love radar" constantly.*
- you are reinforcing caring messages week after week.

Imagine how blessed your spouse feels when week after week you are moving towards them with a reminder that they are still "the one for you" and you love them. Giving is one of those concepts that come very easy in the beginning of the relationship, but it is easy to begin to neglect.

Giving impacts you as well as the one you love. Research has suggested there is an emotional and chemical reaction inside the giver that benefits the giver. I say it like this: *when you give, your own heart gets bigger.* You will fall more in love with your spouse when you make a conscious decision to give to your spouse on a weekly basis. I have never met anyone who has bought a gift for their spouse on a weekly basis and come into my office and said, "I have fallen out of love with my spouse."

I frequently have people come in and say, "I just don't feel it anymore." I will ask them, *when was the last time, you gave your spouse a gift*?

They usually say, "I can't remember."

Another question that I ask on a regular basis is, "If I could give you a magical pill that would cause you to fall back in love with your spouse, would you take the pill?"

When they say *yes*, I tell them the magic pill is *giving*. Giving on a weekly basis will help you experience love in the relationship. Your giving will create the loving feelings. Frequently the feelings are not present because you have stopped taking the loving actions.

What kind of gifts should you give? The gifts do not have to be expensive. They must be thoughtful. On a weekly basis ask yourself the question, "What kind of gift would convey how much I love my spouse?" The gift needs to convey that you are thinking about your spouse, and they matter to you. It can be extravagant, or it can be simple. The important thing is that you are coming inbound on your spouse on a weekly basis with a tangible gift that says, *You matter to me*.

Let your relationship become known as "Oh, you are the couple that exchanges gifts every week!" I have always joked some people don't give on Valentine's Day and anniversaries, but Jennifer and I give on Martin Luther King Jr's birthday, Harry Truman's birthday, Ground Hog Day and April Fool's Day. Every day that is marked by any kind of potential holiday is a day to celebrate your love. Why would you reserve celebrating your love and marriage to just a few days a year? I tell my marriage coaching clients there are only 52 weeks in a year. Why not celebrate all 52 of them?

I can hear someone saying,

"Won't this feel forced or contrived?" or,

"Doesn't giving gifts on a weekly basis get old?" or,

"Doesn't it take the special nature of giving away?" or,

"It feels very materialistic."

Initially, when you start to give in this fashion, it may feel forced or contrived. It may feel as if you are only doing this because you were told to do it. It may feel contrived if your relationship is broken and you really don't feel like giving. Do it anyway. In short order it will no longer feel this way. I challenge couples to give this way for 12 weeks. Reserve judgment until after the twelve weeks.

I have never had anyone take this 12-week challenge and come back and say, "No, this did not work for me." In terms of taking the special nature of giving away, giving was never supposed to be special. Giving is supposed to be second nature. Your spouse is special, not the giving. Put the focus on your special spouse and give to them on a weekly basis. Materialistic? First, the gifts don't have to be expensive. The key is not the financial value of the gift. The power behind the gift is the thought behind it and the message behind the gift.

The message behind the gift is "You matter to me. I give because I love you." Again, the gift can be as simple as a candy bar or as extravagant as a new car or vacation. Don't get caught up in the financial price tag attached to the gift.

A final word of warning about gift giving. To illustrate this point, let me introduce you to Bob and Suzy. They had come to my office in crisis. The challenge was that Suzy felt unloved and neglected by her husband Bob. They had been married for twelve years and Suzy accused Bob of being relationally lazy. Bob was oblivious that anything was wrong in the relationship. He thought things were going great until his wife threated him with divorce and insisted on coming to see me. I gave them several things to work on, as well as this assignment of giving on a weekly basis.

Two weeks later when they came to my office, Suzy reported that things had indeed been better. Bob had made great strides in dating, talking, and touching, but his gift giving demonstrated a continued attitude of laziness. One of Bob's gifts was a $50.00 visa gift card that he simply handed to her. A second gift was a gift that he picked up at the store. He brought it home and pitched it to her (receipt and price tag still on the gift and in the bag) and said, "Here is your gift." Hmmm.

When you give the gift, put some thought in how you will be presenting the gift. Be certain to not just fling it at your spouse. *The presentation of the gift really matters*. Don't just throw it at your spouse in the store-bought bag as if you were giving dog food or groceries. You are presenting a present to your spouse. Present it in a manner that says this gift is thoughtful and valuable. Further demonstrate your love as you are presenting the gift to your spouse.

Be Present...Spend Quality Time with the One You Love

In addition to giving presents on a weekly basis, PHENOMENAL MARRIAGES are intentional about giving presence to one another. To give the gift of presence is to help with chores, children, and other logistical issues that couples tend to in running the home. Frequently these logistical issues are relegated to just one person in the household. This can sometimes lead to resentment and the feeling the other person is not sharing their fair share of the load. To mitigate against this, it is critical that you are communicating about these issues on a regular basis. When it comes to the children, it is often a stay-at-home parent who is responsible for the watershed of the responsibilities. This works, but the parent who is not staying at home must be intentional about giving the gift of presence to balance this out. The best way to do this is to have agreed upon roles and expectations.

One of the habits you can get into is the habit of having meals together on a weekly basis. It is ideal if you can eat together on a nightly basis, but even if you need to start with a once-a-week scenario, this begins to make things better. The key operative is that you sacrifice and give to spend time with one another. It may mean putting your sweatpants on and joining your spouse in the yard or the garage. Or, it could be rolling up your sleeves and doing the dishes. Regardless of what you are doing, you are giving the gift of presence to each other. It is one more way to say, "I love you, and what is important to you is important to me."

Giving the gift of presents and presence can revolutionize your marriage. You will be amazed at how this begins to change the relationship. Make this a high priority for you and your spouse as you launch into the future. This works for great marriages, and even marriages that are not so great.

Action Steps from Chapter 9

1. Have a discussion with your spouse about the role gift giving played in your home growing up and the role that it has had in your marriage to this point.
2. Talk about the types of gifts that you like to receive. Ask questions about the types of gifts your spouse enjoys.
3. Share about the role of intentional presence has played in your marriage to this point. What are some ways you can improve this area of your marriage?
4. Go to www.FromRoommatesToSoulmates.org to get a list of gift giving ideas.

CHAPTER 10

Arguing and Conflict Resolution

THE MERRIAM WEBSTER *Dictionary* defines the word fight as follows: "to use weapons or physical force to hurt someone, to defeat the enemy; to struggle in battle or physical combat, to contend in battle or physical combat, to use words and arguing to overcome others.[11]" The goal of fighting is to get the upper hand. With this definition, I find the following marriage nuggets to be amazing and ridiculous.

- "Fighting is good for the relationship."
- "If you don't fight, you must not be communicating."
- "Great relationships have their fair share of arguing."
- "Our relationship is strong enough that we should be able to withstand a good fight."
- "The best part of fighting is making up."

Have you ever heard any of these relationship lies? There are many people who believe and teach that fighting is a healthy part of a phenomenal marriage. Couples are encouraged to fight fairly. Couples who do not fight are frequently perceived as being in denial or not tuned into the relationship. I wish I was given a quarter for every time a couple comes into my office and says, "Our problem is that we never fought." Their perception is that if they had had knockdown, drag out fights, then maybe they would not be sitting in my office. It is simply not true. You can have a Phenomenal Marriage without fighting. In fact, I would assert that to have a Phenomenal Marriage, you must get a handle on the fighting, arguing, and bickering that occurs in the relationship.

Notice I did not say you cannot have a phenomenal marriage without conflict. All marriages will have conflict. Conflict occurs when our expectations are not met by our spouse. *Every marriage is going to experience conflict.* There are always going to be issues, circumstances, and outcomes that have the potential to disappoint or fall short of our expectations. When this happens, we always have three options.

We have the choice to 1) solve the conflict, 2) ignore the conflict (conflict avoidance), or 3) fight. Our conflict resolution technique is frequently a learned behavior. For many of us, we learned our conflict resolution skills from our parents. If our parents were conflict avoiders, we tend to become conflict avoiders. If our parents were fighters, we tend to become a fighter. The challenge with conflict avoiding and fighting is that they never adequately solve the conflict. Conflict avoiding and fighting lead to a disconnect in the relationship.

Conflict avoidance in a relationship is usually rooted in fear. Conflict avoiders generally have three fears.

Their first fear is a 1) fear of creating a fight. They are so afraid of fighting that they make the decision to ignore their disappointments. They basically suck it up. The problem with sucking it up is that eventually there is so much unresolved conflict inside of the person that it begins to impact the relationship.

2) The second fear that conflict avoiders have is that if they express their disappointment or dissatisfaction, their spouse will no longer love them. They are afraid that by expressing their true feelings, their spouse will be angry, love them less, and somehow create even more pain.

3) The third fear that conflict avoiders have is that their expressing their disappointment and dissatisfaction will not make a difference. It is the thought that this situation is not going to change, so what difference does it make. It is an apathetic "why bother" attitude that leads to apathy in the relationship. Conflict avoidance is not an appropriate way to manage the conflict in your marriage because the conflict never gets solved.

Fighting is not an effective conflict management tool in the relationship. One of the reasons is that it is biologically impossible to connect and fight at the same time. When we fight, our brain releases a chemical that fires on the back side of our brain. The back part of our brain is the most primitive part of the brain. It has also been called the reptilian brain. This part of the brain has two primary functions: *fight or flight.*

When we find ourselves in extremely stressful or angry states, our reaction is to fight or run. The challenge is that neither one of these options are conducive to connecting with your partner. It is impossible to solve conflict by utilizing the back part of the brain. The thinking part of the brain is in the frontal lobes. When we fight, we are accessing the part of the brain that is ineffective in conflict or problem resolution.

Another reason fighting and arguing is so incredibly damaging to our connection is that frequently when we are in these heightened states of emotional darkness, we end up saying and doing things that hurt our partner. These words and actions damage the quality of our connection. Again, it is impossible to connect and confront simultaneously.

Moving Beyond our Fight or Flight Responses

Make a list. When I work with couples in crisis, frequently I have them make a list of the things, issues, and triggers that have led to fighting in the past. If they are having a hard time with this exercise, I tell them to make a list of the last five arguments. When we look at the list together, usually they are issues that have been present in the relationship for a very long time. The truth is most couples do not solve their problems. They simply fight about them but never resolve them. I liken it to a great big pepper shaker over their lives. They are constantly being peppered with these issues, but they never solve them; they simply argue about them.

Refuse to confront for a period of time. After the couple has made the list of these issues, I have them make a commitment that for the next seven days, they will not deal with any of the issues. They are instructed to table the issues and focus only on connecting for the next seven days. It is amazing what happens when couples who have fought every day for years make a commitment to go seven days without fighting. They come back into my office, and they feel like newlyweds. Sometimes they report they have not felt this in love since before they were married.

> **If your marriage is in crisis, focus on re-establishing your connection before you begin to tackle the problems.**

The challenge with traditional marriage therapy is that it generally starts with the problem solving or conflict resolution without reestablishing a connection.

Sometime ago, I had the opportunity to meet William Ury. William Ury is a Harvard professor, bestselling author, anthropologist, and a negotiation expert. Ury's bestselling book, *Getting to Yes* is a classic in terms of conflict resolution[12]. William Ury has been hired by the Unites States government to help solve civil wars in foreign countries. I have found that the principles that he utilizes in these high-powered conflict situations also work in marriages. I have adopted and tweaked his approach to conflict resolution and found that it has really been effective in helping couples quit fighting and start connecting. I call it the Balcony Approach to conflict resolution. It is a six-step process that can help you solve your conflict situations once and for all so that you do not need to continue to fight.

The Balcony Approach to Conflict Resolution

The first step to solving conflict is to adopt the belief that every problem always has a solution. So often we buy into the lie that our problems are unique, too entrenched, too old or too deep to be solved. We may say things like, "We have been fighting about this for years, there is no solution" or "We just have to accept that we disagree, there is no hope for this situation." These statements are simply not true. There is always a solution. Every problem that you face can be solved. Accepting this belief is the first principle of the balcony approach to conflict resolution. You will never solve a problem that you do not believe you can solve.

The next step to solving conflict is to understand that you will never solve a problem from an emotional place. It is impossible to solve problems when you are in a heightened emotional state. When we are in that heighted emotional state, our brain releases a chemical that fires in the reptilian portion of our brain. Recall, this part of the brain is good for two things, fighting or running. Unfortunately, most couples try to solve their conflict from this emotionally heightened place and all they end up doing is fighting more. Scientist in the anger management field say that it takes this part of the brain a good twenty minutes to get back to a normal state where you can actually solve your problems. Since you cannot solve your problems in a heighted state, you would be better served not even to try. Learn strategies and techniques to table your conflict when you are angry. The second reality of this Balcony Approach to conflict resolution is...

You will never solve your problems when you are in a heightened state of anger, distress, or frustration.

Next, *create a time and space set aside to solve the conflict*. I call this process "going to the balcony." Set intentional time aside where your goal is to focus on the conflict and problems in the relationship that need to be solved. For Jennifer and I, we will spend time in front of our fireplace or on our back deck. Whenever we have conflict, we take it to the balcony by going to one of these two places. We arrive at these places with a great deal of hope and certainty that whatever the situation or problem is, we will be able to solve it in the balcony.

Then, *sit down together in the balcony place and begin to look at the problem*. The most important element at this point is that you are very calm, not anxious or fighting, and ready to solve the conflict. I have couples close their eyes, hold hands, and imagine that they are climbing the steps to a balcony in a theatre. They take their seats next to each other in the front row of their balcony seats. When they open their eyes, they see a great big stage with a red curtain. The image I always share is the image of the two old guys in the balcony from the Muppet show. When the red curtain opens, there is a table with a black cloth in the middle of the stage. Sitting on this table is the problem or conflict that the couple has been facing. For many couples, it is the first time they have considered the issue outside of their heads. They are looking down at the problem, getting a completely different perspective of the issue. From this perspective, they can accurately define the problem. Frequently the problem is not the issue that initially presented itself. You can uncover the real issue by asking, "What is the real problem here?" or "What is really going on?"

Now it's time to *make the decision that you are going to be hard on the problem and soft on people.* What generally happens in conflict and fighting is that we go soft on the problem, never actually solving it, and we go hard on people. Make the decision to go hard on the problem and soft on people. You will discover that this approach is softer, and it really works. With this approach, no one gets beat up and the problem gets attacked.

The final step is to *come up with three possible resolutions.* A couple's work is not done until they have three possible solutions. Usually what happens when we are fighting is we quickly come up with two possible solutions. Her solution and his solution. The power behind this approach is that the couple must always come up with a third possible solution. I have found that usually it is this third solution that ends up solving the problem. The reason this approach has been so incredibly effective is because it helps couples get on the solution side of their conflict from a non-emotional, non-fighting angle.

Every relationship and every marriage will have conflict. The key to a great marriage is not great fights, *it is solving and managing the disappointments and unmet expectations.* You will find that when you fight less and communicate more, you connect more often.

Action Steps from Chapter 10

1. Discuss with your partner the three areas of your life together that create the most conflict. How have these issues evolved or changed throughout the history of your relationship.
2. Identify your fighting tendency in terms of fighting or flighting. How has this impacted your marriage.
3. Make the decision to begin using the balcony approach to solve your conflict.

4. Go to www.FromRoommatesToSoulmates.org for 5 more ideas on how to reduce and manage conflict in your relationship.

CHAPTER 11
Protecting the Marriage

WHEN YOU HAVE something of great value, your natural inclination is to protect it. For most of us, our most expensive assets are our homes and cars. For this reason, most of us have homeowner's insurance and car insurance. Our most precious asset is our marriage. Unlike our cars and homes, our spouse is not replaceable. In the same way we protect our financial assets, we must have a plan to protect our marriage. The final element in creating a phenomenal marriage is to have a plan in place to protect the marriage from forces that have the potential to lessen or destroy the marriage. Imagine that your marriage is a beautiful castle located in hostile territory. If you owned a castle in hostile territory, you would most certainly build a moat around it. The moat would serve as an advance warning system and defense against invading enemies. This chapter will provide you with ideas to build a moat around your marriage.

Always putting your marriage first. The first decision you can make to build a moat around your marriage is consciously making the decision to always put your marriage first. Make your relationship with your spouse your number one priority. It may sound obvious or simplistic, but you would not believe the number of people who have been to my office through the years that said, "I am here because I did not make my spouse a priority. Everything else was more important. My children, my work, my friends, my family, and my hobbies took all my time." It is one of the most common things I hear from individuals who come to me after their spouse has confessed, they want a divorce. My clients wished they had made their marriage their number one priority. This simple decision can save you and your marriage. Children, work, friends, family, and hobbies are all good things, but whenever they become more important than your spouse or your marriage, your marriage is in trouble. All these outside sources will at times press against your marriage, jockeying for the number one position. Sometimes we can find ourselves upside down in terms of the time or the emotional energy we are giving to these things. When this happens, we need to reprioritize and make changes to protect our marriage immediately.

The most difficult of these outside forces that jockey for number one tend to be our children and our extended families. Many of us were raised by parents who taught us that our number one priority should be our children. We were told to focus on the kids, and when they are grown and out of the house, then there will be time for you to focus on the marriage. With a divorce rate of 50%, this advice is clearly not working. We absolutely need to make our children a priority. We need to love them, lead them, feed them, clothe them, educate them, encourage them, and teach them to succeed in life. We will have these children in our homes for about 18 to 23 years. The most important thing that we can do for our children is model how they are going to spend the next 70 years.

> **The greatest gift a mother and father can give their children is making their marriage their number one priority.**

By doing this, you model for your children a great marriage and you give them the security of growing up in a home with a mother and father who love each other. I often hear from people, "I just want to focus on the children now, and then we will have the rest of our lives for the two of us". Sadly, the damage that is created by this mindset leaves couples totally disconnected 18 years later. The best strategy is to teach your children that your marriage is your number one priority.

One other note about small children is that sometimes families get into the habit of letting their small children sleep in bed with them. This is very unhealthy for your children, and especially unhealthy for your marriage. Your bed should be off limits to your children. I realize that sometimes it is easier to just let the kids stay in the bed rather than fighting with them to sleep in their own beds. The problem is this will have a negative impact on your marriage down the road, and it will be harder for you to get them to sleep in their own bed later. One effective strategy is to tell them that, if they must, they can sleep on the floor at the end of the bed, but they are not to sleep in the bed. This will happen for a few nights, but before long they will begin to sleep in their own bed. Consult with your pediatrician about additional strategies to help your child sleep in their own bed.

The second most difficult outside force that jockeys for number one tends to be our extended families. Sometimes we cling to our family of origin, and we don't fully lean into our marriage. With an aging generation and the frequency of children now taking care of their parents, this has become even more challenging. While we must take care of our extended families, and family relationships are extremely important, they can never be more important than our relationship with our spouse. You may have to establish healthier boundaries in terms of extended family members. You may have to enlist the help of siblings or hire outside help. Draw a line in the sand and talk with your spouse about what is acceptable and what is not acceptable. It may take a while but, for the sake of your marriage, it will be worth having healthy boundaries. After you have established these boundaries, have the conversation with your extended family. It is never too late to establish healthy boundaries.

Protect from affairs. Some of the forces that the marriage needs protecting from on the surface look very healthy and good. The challenge with these forces is that they start off very innocently, but eventually an emotional attachment and dependency is formed that does not serve the marriage well. These outside forces can become what are called emotional affairs. There are two types of emotional affairs, romantic and non-romantic. Nonromantic affairs happen when people have an emotional affair with their children, their work, their friends, their hobbies, and with other family members. An emotional affair is when a spouse ends up giving to someone else or something else what they should be giving to their spouse. Whenever the object of your affection and attention has more weight than what you are giving your spouse, you are in danger of having an emotional affair. Sometimes a spouse will spend years focusing solely on their children and they end up neglecting their spouse. Sometimes a spouse will spend the watershed of their time with their friends or with their work, neglecting their spouse in the process. Regardless, these misplaced affections are damaging to the relationship.

Some strategies that have helped people combat emotional affairs is to realize that the most important person is your spouse. Keep them consistently in the number one position. Secondly, when you discover that something is slipping into that number one slot, stop immediately. There is nothing worth the cost of a failed marriage. Talk to your spouse about it. Include them in the conversations. Be certain to be doing all the other things that have been discussed in this book.

The second type of affair is the romantic emotional affair. Usually these start off innocently. Most physical affairs do not start in the bedroom. They start outside the bedroom, doing the things that cause connection.

Affair Proof Your Marriage

To affair proof your marriage, you have to have healthy boundaries in terms of people of the opposite sex. Do you remember the things that lead to deep connection in your marriage? They are talking, touching, dating, and giving. These four things are always present at the start of any affair. Affairs start when people begin to 1) talk, 2) touch, 3) give, and 4) spend time with other people. For this reason and to affair proof your marriage, you must have a predetermined strategy to manage talking, touching, giving, and spending time with people of the opposite sex. Just realizing these four things lead to connection can serve you well in safeguarding your marriage. As a general rule, reserve touching of any kind for your spouse. Apart from work, your primary playmate should be your spouse. Talk to your work colleagues during work hours, but when you are home let that be your family time.

When boundaries have been crossed, it does not mean that the marriage relationship needs to end. I have found that when three elements are in place it increases the likelihood that the marriage will survive. The challenge is that these three things work synergistically so all three of them must be in place. If one of them are missing it lessens the chance of healing and reconciliation. The three things are:

- Is the affair ended?
- Is there remorse?
- Is there a plan to move forward with a marriage-helping professional?

Unfortunately, couples will be tending to the first two, but refuse to work on taking the marriage to the next level. When this happens things can get better for a while, but quickly you can end up in another affair situation. When all three things are in place, couples have had a great deal of success in overcoming the affair. When these three things are not in place, it can be much more difficult to survive the affair.

Never threaten divorce. Don't use the "D" word. Another strategy to safeguard your marriage is to never threaten divorce. Decide as a couple that divorce is not going to be an option. Eliminate it as a possibility for your marriage. Stop saying, focusing on it and threatening divorce. Instead, adopt the belief that your marriage is going to be great. Adopt the belief that you deserve a phenomenal marriage, and it is coming your way. Adopt the belief that no matter how bad things may get relationally, the two of you can work through it. Adopt the belief system that says we can always get help and there is always hope. The best time to tap into these mindsets is before there is a marital crisis.

Always speak life over your spouse and about your spouse. I tell people to imagine that their marriage has ears. Everything you say about your marriage has tremendous power over the quality of the marriage. When you talk about your spouse to others, never talk negatively. Only say things that are building up your spouse and the marriage. Be positive when you talk about your spouse. Be positive when you are talking to your spouse. Let them know that you have a phenomenal marriage. Let them know that you are committed to your spouse. This is especially true with extended family members and friends. Never complain to your family or friends about your spouse. If you do, you will forgive your spouse, but your family and friends begin to keep a list of grievances against your spouse that is very hard to recover from. Sadly, many divorces are driven by people outside of the marriage who have formed negative opinions about one of the spouses. In a day and age where divorce is common, when you have spoken negatively about your spouse, you are inviting negative feedback about saving your marriage. Make the decision to speak only positively about your marriage.

What about talking about my marriage issues with others? You might be thinking, what if my spouse is being a jerk? What if the marriage is in a crisis? Am I supposed to lie to people? I would never recommend that you lie, but your marriage is sacred, and your marital conflict should be private. If this describes your situation and you are asked, simply say that you are working through some things, but you love your spouse and you value your marriage. If you need to complain or vent, seek the help of a professional that can help you create a plan to fix the problems. No one ever complained their way to a better marriage. Instead of complaining to your family and friends, make the decision that you are going to take the energy that you would spend in doing this and place that energy into getting help for your marriage. The truth is that long after you and your spouse are reconciled and doing well, all the people that you complained to will not have forgotten nor forgiven your spouse.

Grow together as a couple. The final thing to do to safeguard your marriage is to have a plan to continue to grow as a couple. I recommend that couples develop a relationship growth plan. The growth plan should include weekly, monthly, and yearly activities to ensure that your relationship continues to grow and thrive. On a weekly basis, conduct the weekly business meeting. This was discussed early in this book. This meeting is where you are intentionally checking in and talking about the week and the relationship. During this meeting, reflect on the week. Look at your marriage manifesto and ask whether this statement accurately reflects who you were as a couple in the last seven days. If you find that you are off track, don't fight about it. Come up with a plan to get right back on track this week. Make commitments on a weekly basis to improve on the areas that are not working.

Consider reading two or three marriage enrichment books a year. There are so many great marriage enrichment books. If you are not one for reading books, consider getting a book on tape. There are also many video options. The important thing is that you are making your marriage such a high priority that you are constantly looking for ways to improve and keep it passionate. Consider going on at least one marriage retreat a year. Once a year get away for the purpose of strengthening your marriage. If you have a religious affiliation, you may want to check and see if they have offerings for marriage enrichment. The possibilities for your growth plan can be endless. Have fun with it and be intentional. Remember, having a phenomenal marriage is a lifelong journey that requires work and effort. Invest in growing your marriage. The payoff will be that you have safeguarded your marriage.

If you want to have a PHENOMENAL MARRIAGE, you want to have these strategies in place to protect the marriage from outside forces. When you build a moat around your marriage, you definitely safeguard it from the things that lead people into divorce court. The time to get the plan in place is before you have the issues and before you are in a crisis. Decide to start building the moat today.

Action Steps from Chapter 11

1. Commit to making your marriage your number 1 priority. If you have children talk about beliefs, you had growing up in terms of what the highest priority should be and how these beliefs may have changed because of this chapter.
2. Discuss the strategies for building a moat around your marriage. Which strategies resonated with you? Where do your opinions and ideas differ?
3. Go to www.FromRoommatesToSoulmates.org to get additional resources to help you to continue to grow your relationship.

Epilogue

DYING FROM A broken heart is not just a cliché in movies and romantic novels. There is a medical term for it, called Takotsubo cardiomyopathy. This is an acute heart failure that can be triggered by emotional stress. Takotsubo cardiomyopathy is known as "broken heart syndrome". My family recently experienced this condition. My parents, Donald and Kayleen Rispoli, were married for 57 years. They met when they were 16 and 14 at a Halloween Party in New Castle Pa. From that day on, except for my dad's service in the United States Marine Corp, they were inseparable. We always thought that my Dad would pass before my Mom, so we were shocked when my Mom developed pneumonia and passed away suddenly in June of 2021. My Dad was devastated. Even though my dad was relatively healthy in June of 2021, he passed away seven months later in January of 2022. My Dad had lost hope. He lost his reason for living. He died of a broken heart.

In my work with struggling couples, I have found that when they come into my office, they are looking for two things. First, they are looking for a toolbox to improve their marriage. Secondly, they are looking for hope. They are looking for a reason to not let the relationship die. They want to believe that things can and will get better. I hope in this book you have found a toolbox to help create a phenomenal marriage. I hope it helps you create a phenomenal marriage not by drift or by default, but by design. I guarantee if you do the things that are outlined in this book you will have a phenomenal marriage. My goal in writing the book has been to very practically lay out the steps needed to create a beautiful soul mate relationship.

I want to conclude this book with a few words about hope. One of the things that I tell all my clients when they start their journey with me is to tap into hope like they never have before. Hope is the common denominator behind every marriage reconciliation or restoration that I have ever seen. When we lose hope, we either quit or we sabotage. In your quest to create a phenomenal marriage you can't quit. So don't lose hope.

There is a famous but controversial study that was conducted in the 1950's by Curt Richter. Curt Richter was a Harvard Graduate and a scientist with John Hopkins University. Curt's experiments focused on how long it takes rats to die from drowning. His hypothesis was that introducing rats to hope would increase their survival times. He conducted his experiments by placing rats into buckets filled with water and seeing how long they survived. He introduced a range of variables into the experiment that yielded some interesting results. Here is what he found, rats who are apparently known for their strong swimming skills, lasted an average of 15 minutes before drowning. In a second experiment, Richter rescued the rats when he saw them begin to stop swimming and sink. He took the rats out, dried them off and gave them a period of rest. Later Richter put these same rescued rats back into the bucket of water. The results were amazing. All the rats swam longer than 15 minutes. In fact, they swam for nearly 60 hours. What made the difference? How was it possible to go from swimming for 15 minutes to swimming for 60 hours? The rats who swam for 60 hours assumed that they could be rescued. They had hope. These rats viewed their situation as temporary. When we are hopeful that our situation can change, we can achieve extraordinary things.

What do drowning rats have to do with turning roommates into soulmates? You may have experienced some difficulties upstream, but don't give up and don't lose hope. The women I met on the plane who I mentioned at the beginning of this book did not believe it was possible to turn roommates into soul mates. The truth is she had lost hope. When we lose hope, we can throw in the towel. It is finished. But if you can hold on just a little while longer and tap into hope like you never have before, you can definitely, not only save your marriage, but you can also create a soul mate situation. That's my life mission.

Thank you for taking the time to read this book! I am so honored to have had the opportunity to take this journey from roommates to soul mates with you. If I have helped you not lose hope and work hard to create a phenomenal marriage, this book has achieved its purpose. Share it with a friend. My life's mission is to help save a million marriages one marriage at a time. You deserve to have a phenomenal marriage! Don't quit, keep hope alive and keep loving!

Sincerely,
David Rispoli

Endnotes

CHAPTER 1

1. YouGov Today, 2021). "Do Americans believe in the idea of soulmates?" Retrieved from https://today.yougov.com/society/articles/34094-soulmates-americans/

2. Plato. Symposium. Trans. Alexander Nehamas and Paul Woodruff. Indianapolis: Hackett, 1989.

3. McQuilken, Robert. "Robert McQuilken Resignation Speach." YouTube, uploaded by 88NewsWorld, 5 March 2018, www.youtube.com/watch?v=yka-bs2xNQs.

CHAPTER 2

4. Anthony Robbins, Awaken the Giant Within (New York: Free Press, 1991).

CHAPTER 4

5. Katy Milkman, Ph.D. (2020). How to Change. New York: Random House.

CHAPTER 5

6. Dobson, Emerson. Love and Respect: The Love She Most Desires; The Respect He Desperately Needs. Thomas Nelson, 2004.

7. Harley, Willard F. *His Needs, Her Needs* (p. 84). Baker Publishing Group. Kindle Edition.

8. Proverbs 15:1 NLT

CHAPTER 9

9. Sheryl Paul, M.A. *HUFFPOST,* 12.15.2012. https://www.huffpost.com/entry/love-is-a-verb_b_1940731

10. Chapman, Gary. The 5 Love Languages: The Secret to Love That Lasts. Moody Publishers, 2015.

CHAPTER 10

11. Merriam-Webster's Collegiate Dictionary, 1999

12. Ury, William. (2011). Getting to yes: Negotiating agreement without giving in. Penguin Books

What People are Saying about David Rispoli (The Marriage Coach)

Dave is an amazing coach! He has truly helped us to evolve our marriage and guided us to a place where we feel deeply connected. Dave helps you find the reasons why you married your spouse and takes it back to the basics. We would recommend him to anyone looking to get the most out of their marriage!

-Amanda D.

My husband and I really enjoy working with David. From day one he offered a money-back guarantee and we never once thought we didn't get our money's worth.

During each and every session we have been provided with new tools to help us communicate and grow closer! From physical to spiritual connection we have never been better! We always walk out so proud of our growth.

I highly recommend anyone in a relationship to visit with David at least once...whether you think you have issues or not. He provides great tools to get your marriage to the best it's ever been!

-Kelly D.

I found Dave through a random Google search. My husband and I were going through some issues that I felt were pretty unique to us and complicated. I had no idea what I was looking for in a marriage counselor, but I kept coming back to Dave. I really liked his story and the incredibly positive, seemingly "too good to be true" reviews. My husband agreed to go talk to him and I made the call. Dave called me personally the next day. Despite the limited information I gave him, he seemed very confident he could help us. Dave is an exceptional mediator. He helped me to really hear my husband. This required humility and understanding on my part. He has given us so many tools to build on and keep our marriage strong, I truly believe no one else could have helped us like Dave did. He 100% is in this business to save marriages.

-Nina S.

If you are sick and tired of being sick and tired David is the one to see! Can't believe how kind and compassionate of a person he is and how comfortable he is to talk to! Dave has a different approach to marriage counseling by being a coach and he walks beside you with positivity and hope while you are on the journey to heal. He has so many insights and can help transform your marriage to a level that is incredible. I would recommend him to anyone. He can truly be a lifesaver. Thank you, David.

-Gayle H.

Roommates to Soulmates. How many of us are in this type of marriage? The 100% money-back guarantee speaks volumes about how devoted Dave is to saving 100 marriages. There are so many marriage testimonies about couples that were checked out. I met Dave in a networking group and I was that spouse that was checked out of her marriage. It takes a couple to save a broken marriage but it starts with one person who is willing to be coachable and is ready to hit the reset button to restore it.

Dave offers hope, resources, positive feedback, and experience and he is a great listener! I would highly recommend him!

-Tracy M.

Finding Dave has been the best thing to happen to our relationship, we were very much on the edge of going our separate ways. Dave has given us the tools to help us learn to communicate more effectively and we are rebuilding the relationship we had in the beginning. We are very thankful for Dave and would recommend him 100% to anyone needing help to guide their relationship/marriage.

-Kristi W.

David is an awesome counselor/coach. I like that he is straight and forward about addressing issues. I like that he does not sugarcoat anything. The assignments that he gives really do work. I think that if you are the couple looking to get back on track or as David calls it hitting the reset button, he would be the person that could definitely help you do that.

-Wilhelmina J.

No need to wait until marriage to visit! We've been visiting David with STL Marriage Coaching for several months while we've been dating. There were no major 'issues' (as people like to say), but more so wanted to ensure we had a strong foundation for our relationship before marriage. David has made it easier to have some of those 'hard' conversations. He also doesn't force us into uncomfortable conversations until we're ready. He helped us set up some best practices to take home and begin integrating them into our daily lives which has tremendously helped our communication and happiness!

I would HIGHLY recommend David with STL Marriage Coaching to anyone — whether you're in a committed relationship, looking for pre-marital counseling after an engagement, or already married.

-Mystle S.

The stresses of life (child, loss of parent, work) had slowly come down on us and began to creep into our marriage. We were once so connected, but then found ourselves constantly fighting and not coming to an agreement on anything anymore. We both agreed something had to change and were willing to see someone outside of our support circle to get an unbiased look at what was going on. After the first appointment, we were shell-shocked, or at least I was! Dave's non-standard approach to helping couples works. You may feel you are in a place where you can't get help, but rest assured if you are willing to take Dave's advice and put it into action he can help your marriage. I highly suggest Dave, he is a great coach and has very valuable resources to help your relationship. I will continue to suggest him to anyone I know who is going through a difficult time in their marriage. We all have hard times, it is how you deal with them that counts! Now go make your appointment with him.

-Kara K.

My husband and I requested Dave's professional counseling because, after 23 years of marriage, we had entered into a stale place. We loved each other but found we kept re-hashing old wounds and falling into familiar hurtful patterns that were eroding our happiness. We did not want to get a divorce. But we did want to improve our relationship and how we behaved toward each other. Enter Dave Rispoli. He has started every session with tools to improve our connection, communication, and intimacy. The focus has been on building trust and closeness again, not picking bones with each other. We are using the tools Dave has recommended and are seeing a positive impact. Dave's calm and non-judgemental approach is very much welcome. It is exactly what we needed. I highly recommend Dave's counseling service for anyone needing to repair their marriage or if you just want to take your relationship to a deeper level.

-**Ellen G.**

Dave is an amazing marriage coach/ counselor. With a non-traditional approach to helping any couple seeking to fix or even just improve their marriage. He truly cares about the institution and making sure you and your partner have the tools needed to be successful. From the lowest part of our relationship to being in a great loving place, it was Dave that guided us there with zero judgment and a real plan. Thank you Dave for giving us our love and appreciation for each other back. I 100% believe he could help anyone.

-**Mike S.**

My fiancé & I started seeing David a few months ago. We're getting married in September and have been best friends for over 20 years. Our communication was destroying us. We were butting heads every which way, crossing boundaries, and forgetting to spend time together.. I'm not sure what had changed or where the pressure was coming from but David helped us get back on track! We are so in love and hated what was going on between the two of us. This isn't traditional counseling sessions and each time we went we came out feeling invincible. He helped guide us and helped us remember why we fell in love in the first place. We practice the tools he gave us, daily. The fighting, arguing, being against each other...it's all stopped since we met Dave. We can't thank him enough. If you're even slightly thinking about going to see him, just do it. You won't regret it.

-Lacey M.

Dave is passionate about helping couples get to the best place in their relationship.

My wife and I had been to "marriage counselors" in the past but they didn't provide any lasting tools for growing our relationship. Dave's coaching method gave us concrete tasks and goals that helped us get from the darkest to the brightest place of our nine years of marriage, without either of us feeling ganged up on or beaten down while rehashing past mistakes. Dave has given us the tools to keep our marriage healthy and growing in the future, and I look forward to those years with confidence and excitement. If I could give six stars, I would.

-Jeff R.

I wish there were more stars available. Where do I start, I guess from the start. My husband and I were really at our lowest points and needed immediate help!!! We were against all odds, in a fairly new marriage, and now new parents. Nonetheless, before throwing in the towel I started praying and searching for a therapist to then discover scary reviews, virtual sessions, and closed-ended results.

Though I knew it was urgent, I went back to the drawing board and continued praying, and a few days later came I across The Marriage Coach. I remember saying to myself hmm, we really need a counselor, not a coach but at the same time I was willing to try something new. Along with faith, prayer, and his amazing reviews we decided to give it a try..... Let me start with this, for the couple debating financially...you must invest in yourself and your marriage IF you really want it to elevate. That was us too, can we really afford this I remember thinking but divorce is so much more so we stepped out on faith and it was THE BEST DECISION EVER. David is truly a blessing. He is anointed and will bless way more than millions of lives.

Through his program not only are my husband and I reconnected as one but we have both grown individually. We found ourselves excited for the next session and challenge. David was open and honest and allowed us to be ourselves. We were able to express deeply our true emotions without having the feeling of needing to beat one another up verbally. It was honestly a transformational experience.

As a person who has tried counseling before, I challenge you to get coached. You will not regret it. Once again for the person reading this whether you are inquiring about marriage, a newlywed, or someone going through hell in marriage LOOK NO FURTHER. Your new beginning starts here. I have been there, so know that I am rooting for you too!

-Opal O.

We found Dave through a friend who met him while traveling on a plane, oddly enough. When my friend found out what was going on for us she strongly recommended Dave and told me that his goal was to "save a million marriages". I was not sure ours could be saved, but for some reason, I decided to email him that night. The very next day, I got a call from a St. Louis number and we connected. I told my husband about the referral and the phone call and he pretty much said we needed to try, "What did we have to lose"? So, we set up our first appointment via Zoom for a few days later on a Friday night. After our first session, we both felt that we were ready to work and Dave was the perfect fit for us.

His approach is focused on the positive and moving forward, but he also encourages us to communicate about how we got to the place we were at, but he is sure to bring it back around to positives. Dave helped us to focus on what we need to do to not only heal but to make our marriage better than it has ever been and to find each other again in a new way.

We are both definitely working together, better than we ever have, and are using the tools that Dave helped us to develop, every day, to keep moving forward and building a stronger marriage. As we work on ourselves, we are finding things that we forgot about and rediscover each other and ourselves. We are sticking with Dave for support and reinforcement to keep us on track, but we know that what we thought was broken forever is now getting better than ever. Thanks again Dave for everything.

-Bonnie S.

My husband and I had been to traditional marriage counselors numerous times throughout our 20-year marriage and spent more money than I care to remember because our insurance didn't cover marriage counseling. After almost every marriage counseling appointment we left the office more angry, frustrated, and hopeless than when we arrived.

When we found St. Louis Marriage Coach David Rispoli, my husband and I were on the verge of a divorce. David helped save our marriage and did it without either of us having to dredge up and relive all our past hurts and failures. Our extremely positive experience with having David as our marriage coach was incredibly refreshing after suffering years of frustration at the hands of the traditional marriage counseling approach.

A marriage counselor generally keeps you stuck in the past and you often end up rehashing old arguments and problems that you can't go back and change or solve, which only leads to further animosity in the relationship. A marriage coach, on the other hand, keeps you focused on the future and gives you concrete and sustainable tips and ideas on how to keep your marriage moving forward instead of looking back at all the past hurt and mistakes.

David is extremely skilled in keeping you forward-focused and redirecting you to keep you moving in a positive direction that will allow you to build the marriage you have always longed for. He continually offers heartfelt encouragement and hope. His positivity is contagious. You simply can't end a session with David feeling anything but renewed hope and positivity, no matter how frustrated, hopeless, and lost you were feeling 60 minutes earlier.

After just one session with David, I could tell this wasn't simply a career for him—it was his passion. David truly has a gift and seizes every opportunity he can to share it with as many people as possible in an attempt to fulfill his goal of saving one million marriages.

Instead of letting you rehash and get stuck in the negativity of the past, which I think becomes a default for couples who have been struggling in troubled marriages, David keeps you focused on learning new skills and implementing effective choices to build a better, more fulfilling marriage with a strong foundation.

David is incredibly empathetic and encouraging and is genuinely invested in seeing your marriage succeed. My only regret is that we didn't find him sooner.

-Sherri C.

David is truly an amazing man! He guided us through a really hard time in our marriage. Within 6 months of seeing David, we bought our home together. Without him, we would not have made it this far. The best investment we've ever made for our family!

-Julie G.

David is absolutely the most phenomenal marriage coach. He not only helped me save my marriage when there was no hope and it was falling apart but he's the most compassionate person who is always available when there are bumps along the road. After trying so many things, he's really the only thing/person that I would recommend for a marriage/relationship journey.

-Teeba A.

When your marriage is struggling it can be a hopeless feeling. Thank God I found David Rispoli. David is a true professional in every sense of the word. He really took the time to get to know me and my wife, both as individuals and as a couple. David really took the time to get to know in depth, the little things about our marriage. He did not once judge us or cast blame on either one of us but rather worked with us to help us become the best versions of ourselves. He has done a great job of coaching us through some very difficult times and helped us to find solutions to problems that have been plaguing our marriage for over 15 years. I can honestly say that I would probably not be married right now if I had not met David when I did. I am right now the happiest I have been in my marriage since the day I said: "I do". Thank you David for all of your hard work, effort, and professionalism you displayed during the course of helping to turn my marriage around.

-Brian C.

St. Louis Marriage COACHING

David Rispoli
Phone: 314-201-8368
David@stlouismarriagecoaching.com
TheMarriageCoach.com

Turning Roommates into Soulmates

Multiple options to best serve you!

- In Office
- Phone
- Video
- Day Long Intensives

David Rispoli is the president and founder of St. Louis Marriage Coaching and is known internationally and throughout the United States as **The Marriage Coach**. He has been coaching individuals, couples, and businesses for the past two decades. He started his coaching business in the corporate world working in the financial planning industry, and today he continues to coach businesses across a myriad of industries. David was trained by world-renowned expert Mort Fertel in the Marriage Fitness approach to saving marriages and still works as one of the Marriage Fitness consultants. During this time, he has helped hundreds of couples from all around the world restore their broken marriages and experience the marriage of their dreams.

David's unique approach to working with couples in crisis absolutely works. He has a positive solution-focused style that gives couples the tools they need to stop fighting, get connected, and create the marriage of their dreams. Couples leave the session with a Marriage Toolbox that works and a real sense of hope.

David has a Bachelor's Degree in Philosophy from Slippery Rock University and completed his graduate work earning three Master's Degrees. He has earned a Master's of Divinity from Gettysburg. He has an MBA in Human Resource Management and a Master's of Science in Leadership. As a former United States Marine, he is highly motivated and mission driven.

Have you lost your connection with your spouse?
Are you living like roommates?
Is your spouse having an affair?
Maybe you have been told "I love you, but I'm not in love with you" or even "I have never loved you".

This does not have to be the final answer.
There is hope for your marriage, and you CAN have the marriage you envisioned.
Turning Roommates Into Soulmates is our passion,
and we see marriages transformed daily. Yours can be next!

Our unique strategy works. That is why we offer a
100% Money Back Guarantee

Learn more about Relationship Coaching or Get Started at:
TheMarriageCoach.com
314-201-8368